GIRLS LIKE YOU

'In your mother you were safe and that was the only time you couldn't get kidnapped and that was the nearest you ever were to any other human being.'

– Edna O'Brien, A Pagan Place

'Words without experience are meaningless.'

– Vladimir Nabokov, Lolita

GIRLS LIKE YOU

The Long Road Back from Bessborough

JACINTA O'CONNELL

Published by
Red Stripe Press

an imprint of

Orpen Press
Upper Floor, Unit B3
Hume Centre
Hume Avenue
Park West Industrial Estate
Dublin 12
Ireland

email: info@orpenpress.com
www.orpenpress.com

Paperback ISBN 978-1-78605-137-0
ePub ISBN 978-1-78605-138-7

Printed in Dublin by SPRINTprint Ltd

For the women of Ireland who were removed from their families, incarcerated in mother and baby homes, separated from their children, whose voices were silenced. May your voices be heard. May your silence be broken.

Acknowledgements

It takes a village. I would like to thank the following people, without whom this work would not have reached completion. Angela Hanley, for your unwavering support and encouragement throughout, for your editorial assistance, your keen eye for detail and your friendship. Thank you to the amazing English Department of All Hallows College. Anthony Draper, Martin McConigley and Brian Dooney – your passion for all things literature lit a fire within me that burns to this day. I could not have picked a worse time to divulge my secret than in the middle of completing an MA thesis. Thank you to Michael Cronin, Sinéad Kennedy and Moynagh Sullivan from the English Department in Maynooth University. Your support during this time was invaluable, your influence far greater than academic. Thank you to the Barnardos Post-Adoption Services in Dublin for your support while I was going through the aftermath of breaking my silence as a birth mother. Thank you to the Fr Hudson's Adoption Support Agency in England whose Trojan work in helping Irish birth mothers is such an important and valuable resource. Thank you Athlone Writers Group for providing the space to share my work. Your ongoing encouragement, feedback and companionship throughout this process has been invaluable. Thank you Rory Duffy for the use of your poem 'Wembley High Road', and for all things pertaining to earthquakes. I would like to thank my family and friends who read over, made suggestions, proofread and basically listened while I regaled them with snippets of my past. Thank you Emma, Ruth, Ger, Adrienne, Martin McConigley, Mary Lennon. I would like to sincerely thank everyone on Professor Aoife Lowry's team in the Day Surgery Ward and at the Symptomatic Breast Clinic, University Hospital Galway. When my writing was interrupted for a medical procedure you were true carers in this time of chaos. I would also like to thank William Quain of Athlone City Photography for resurrecting my old Confirmation photograph when I thought there was no hope of doing so. Finally, a massive thank you to Red Stripe Press. Thank you, Michael Brennan and Eileen O'Brien, for giving me the opportunity to tell my story.

Contents

Introduction

'Memory fills my body as much as blood and bones.'
– Colm Tóibín, *The Testament of Mary*

Memories are strange entities. They are the thickened skin we build our lives around, the hidden vertebrae of our outward existence, until one day a familiar smell, a chance word or a sidelong glance and ... boom! They push their way upwards, erupting in a cacophony of sound and images that cannot be ignored. Sometimes they are as silent and lethal as noxious gas, slowly seeping upwards, almost choking us in their demand for recognition. Some are so carefully buried that only the skill of the professional can help bring them to light. But inevitably they emerge in all their various forms; hesitant nudges, confusing flashbacks or full-blown 'I'm coming through now' memories. They can be misleading, becoming entangled with one another so that places, dates, colours or even names are distorted. As we view our lives through the fractured prism of memory we may wonder if we are going mad. We may question the validity of our memories.

'Is this really who I was back then?'

'Would I have said that? Did I really do those things?'

Sometimes the best thing to do is just give them free rein, allow the dust to settle before beginning the excavation process. It takes courage and a slight touch of madness to peer through the veil of memory and still hold on to ourselves.

My memories of Bessborough House are a kaleidoscope of images, colours, sounds and smells; a collage of faces, voices, rooms, stairs and stone floors. They consist of sensations, like that of falling onto the hard stone floor of the chapel where I landed each morning due to chronic morning sickness. They are the smell of the disinfectant that greeted me when I eventually came around.

'You wouldn't expect someone else to clean up your mess now, would you?'

This was said as I was handed the bucket and mop to clean up the mess I had made, a reminder that this situation I found myself in was a mess of my own making. Years later, when my young children were affected by childhood illnesses, that blended aroma of vomit and disinfectant transported me instantly to the cold stone floor where I had lain prostrate while the nuns continued to offer up the sacrifice of morning Mass for the sins of our souls. Afterwards, the smell of food cooking in the kitchen where I had been put to work awakened a fierce hunger in me, as if every part of my being was crying out to be fed after the physical and psychological rejection of those early mornings. The swish of closing curtains conjures up the movement of the nun's garments as they floated around the various rooms of the building, giving orders or clapping hands to claim attention as they looked down on us lowly bloated sinners from their superior height.

There is nothing quite like the sound of an institution. The muted sobs of women who were separated from the children they had just given birth to mingled with the mumbled prayer that pervaded the house at regular intervals. Ave Marias and Hail Marys fused with condemnation of the graceless sinners who dwelt there. One of my first memories of the house is that of the steps leading up to a large red door. For years I wondered if I had imagined the colour of the door, but when I eventually found the courage to Google an image of the house I realised that this memory was a true one, the door was indeed red. The steps looked smaller, though, and less imposing than I remembered. This is the thing about memory. It is not simply what we saw or experienced that impacts us, but how that experience and the memory of it makes us feel about ourselves. My memories may be hazy at times, even contradictory, but one thing I am sure about is that those steps took me to a threshold that, once crossed, would change my life for ever.

Before Bessborough House I just an ordinary girl, growing up in the Midlands town of Athlone. My siblings and I liked to think of ourselves as townies, and were greatly offended when our Dublin cousins referred to us as 'culchies'. In reality we spent as much time roaming the fields as we did strolling through the town with our parents. The town was smaller then, and when we went uptown with our mother it seemed as if she was always meeting people she knew, always stopping to chat or calling greetings across the street. As we got older we hated having to go with her as it meant standing by while she stopped to talk to people. 'Why can't we just go to town for once and not have to keep stopping?' we would ask. But her response was to tell us to stay quiet and not interrupt.

One of our favourite activities during the summer months was playing in the hay barn. This barn belonged to the father of one of our friends and was situated at the back of the pub he ran. Each summer when the hay was gathered in we held jumping competitions there. From the precarious heights of the building we completed death-defying leaps, trusting the soft hay below to break our fall. It was all great fun until a hint of competition entered the game, with each leap becoming more daring. Then someone would get hurt and what had seemed like a good idea on a warm summer's day ended in tears or fighting, or both. The heated arguments, the tears, the swearing that we would never speak to one another again undermined the innocence of the whole adventure. The fights never lasted long though. We were too busy enjoying our childhood, too busy planning the next great adventure. Before we knew it we were all friends again and played together in the hay barn, until the next skirmish occurred and the whole process would start again.

The price I paid for my time in the hay barn was the annual boil-lancing ritual that was performed by my father every summer without fail. The painful experience of the first time this happened had taught me to ignore the initial symptoms when they began to appear. It had been established that an allergy to hay was the cause and the guilt of ignoring this, coupled with the knowledge of what was to come, strengthened my resolve to hide the swelling growth. 'It's just a pimple,' I would remark casually, hiding my fear as I knew what was in store for me. My father, who also knew what was coming, kept a watchful eye on it. It was so unfair. To be allergic to something that brought so much fun and was so hard to resist. Eventually the boil would become too painful and too engorged with pus to hide or to bear. Then, even though we all knew how this was going to end, the ritualistic dance would begin. My mother's contribution to the process was to boil the kettle in order to sterilise the long darning needle that would be used to puncture the offending carbuncle. At the sight of the needle I would begin to sob hysterically. My father would patiently ask if he could lance the boil, explaining that this was the only way to alleviate the pain. The thought of that boiling hot needle piercing the painful swelling terrified me, but eventually, after much cajoling and some bribery, sweets or ice cream or, better again, money, I would allow him to perform the mini operation. The truth was, that in spite of the pain and fear, I trusted him and believed that he could take the pain away. When it was over, I would swear never to go near the hay barn again. I even kept the promise for a short time, but as summer neared I forgot about the agony of the boils and the red-hot needle and joined my friends to jump into the hay. The result, of course, was the inevitable ritual, which was carried out again and again until a combination of outgrowing the thrill of the hay barn and an aversion to pain eventually brought it to an end. When I look back now I wonder how I allowed myself to go through this experience year after year. But to this day, the smell of freshly cut hay evokes the memory of those days and I can still feel that sense of wild abandonment when I made that first hesitant jump from the top of the barn. There was nothing as exhilarating as the first leap into the unknown. When I was in Bessborough House I remembered that feeling and I remembered the patience and unconditional care of my father. Even though I deliberately disregarded his advice to stay away from the hay, he would still go through the lancing process each year until I grew out of that phase of my life. As I looked down at my swollen belly I knew there was no one to offer that unconditional care now. My father was not here to help with this. I had been thrust out of my comfortable, dependable life. This was a dance I would have to perform on my own.

1

The Early Years

'It was the last day of childhood.'

— Edna O'Brien, *The Country Girls*

Growing up in a small town in the Irish Midlands didn't offer much scope for an exciting life, but in hindsight it seems almost idyllic. Athlone straddles the Connacht and Leinster sides of town, which are divided by the River Shannon. I grew up on the Leinster side and, for as long as I can remember, everyone I knew referred to the area of town across the bridge as 'the far side'. It came as a great shock to realise that people who lived on the Connacht side of town referred to where I lived as 'the far side'. Everyone thought that they were on the near side of town, or the right side. Such are the vagaries of growing up in a town that straddles not just two counties, but two provinces. I have always been conscious of this divide, not just in relation to the geography of where I lived, but in relation to how the division affected my personal life also. My mother came from Galway and my father was an Athlone man, one from Connacht, the other from Leinster. We lived in Athlone, but spent most of the summer months in Galway with our mother. My father loved the river; my mother missed the sea. I can remember trips to the boat-building shed in Payne's Lane where my father would spend what seemed like hours discussing boat-building with the other men there. Would fibreglass hulls replace wooden ones? What was the best shape or structure for a boat? How would she float when launched? My siblings and I found all of this very boring. We were much more interested in when the boat would finally be ready and we would have our first trip on the river. Though we loved those times spent out on the water with him we also discovered a great love of the sea during the summer months in Galway with my mother. This, coupled with the excitement of double-decker buses and the busyness of the city, introduced another element into our lives, and, to this day, I find myself pulled between the river and the sea, the quietness of suburban life and the bustle of the city. Later on, when the cracks began to show in my parents' marriage, there was another divide to contend with. But that is another story. When I was a teenager one of our favourite pastimes was to walk across the white railway bridge that spanned the river and linked the Leinster and Connacht sides of the town. The bridge was frequently used as a shortcut and, as the arches were wider than they seemed at first sight, we had decided to take things a bit further and try to walk across them. When I look back now I can hardly believe that I used to do this. In a way I was straddling the divides of my life full on, impervious to the danger, as the young often are. Though I was unaware of it, there was an important division occurring in Ireland around this time. I was born in 1957 and by the time I reached my thirteenth birthday in 1970 society was beginning to change. This change would happen very slowly in Ireland, too slowly to change my story, but there was a generation rising up who would begin to question the religious and social mores of this time. My story takes place during this period in Ireland, but while the women's movement was active in America and Britain it did not save me from the dictates of the religious and societal morality that pervaded the country at this time and were especially cruel to women.

Growing up in 1960s Ireland meant that we lived our lives through the regimes of home, school and Church. The school calendar dictated our movements just as surely as the seasons of the year did, and as the school calendar was structured around the religious one, it was really the Church that ordained our lives, and often our diet. We attended Mass every Sunday and on holy days and we always knew what was on the menu for Friday's dinner. We fasted before Sunday Mass in order to receive communion and afterwards we would have a big fry-up for breakfast. On Sundays we always had a roast for dinner followed by dessert. Our early years were punctuated by First Confession, Holy Communion and Confirmation. School was where we learned to flex our academic muscles but it was also where we learned to obey and fear the authority of the Church. This was partly down to the unspoken assumption that respect was due to the parish priest whenever he arrived in the classroom and partly down to the cane the nun kept visible at the top of the room. When the priest arrived, often unexpectedly, he would quiz us to see how well we knew our catechism, or ask who had been at Mass that Sunday. As he looked at each one of us we knew that he could see everything and that it was pointless to hide the truth from him. Woe betide anyone who failed the catechism questions, as that would reflect badly on the nun in charge of the class who, after the priest had left, was liable to take out her frustration on the child in question. This very rarely happened to me as I was one of the good girls.

The first major event in my younger years was preparation for First Confession, an event fraught with opportunities to get things wrong. Would I remember when to kneel, sit, stand, what prayers to say, and, above all, would I remember the sins I had learned off by rote for confession? How does a seven-year-old understand what sin is? Well, that was taken care of by the catechism and the nuns. Did you give back cheek to your parents? Did you tell a lie? Did you hit one of your sisters? Or brothers? Did you do something to offend God, who was constantly listening and watching, who saw everything? Was it a venial sin or a mortal one? I can remember being afraid of the darkness of the confession box and whether the sins I had memorised would be good enough for confession. It was all very stressful.

First Confession was closely followed by the next hurdle, First Holy Communion. The anxiety of what should have been a day of celebration was exacerbated by being presented as a class and having to move up and down the church in a certain order. Losing my sense of direction after receiving the body of Jesus, which was now stuck to the roof of my mouth, I couldn't find my way back to my seat. I was terrified that I wouldn't be able to move the 'sacred host'. What would happen if it hit off my teeth? 'Swallow, don't bite.' That was the sacred rule. I had to be directed down the church by the teacher and by the time I got back to my seat and managed to swallow the wafer I was sweating buckets and totally mortified. Once I recovered from this there was the communion breakfast to look forward to. We had to fast overnight before we received communion so we were starving. All decked out in our fine dresses and suits, patent shoes and white socks, we trooped back to the school to have our breakfast feast. I don't remember what was on the menu but you can be sure it wasn't anything that lived up to my mother's Sunday fry-up. After this we were reunited with our families and began the visits to our neighbours and relations to show them how wonderful we looked, and to collect as much money as we could in the process. After the trauma of the whole thing I felt I deserved the money. The afternoon was spent with my parents and siblings. There was no thought of going for a meal or heading to the pub. Things were more low-key back then. A drive to the countryside, more visits, with more exclamations of how beautiful I looked in my mini wedding dress and veil, and more money. This was the way of things back then. This 'treat time' was accompanied by the threat of what would happen to me if I got my dress or good new shoes dirty, as I would have to wear the outfit to school the following Monday to have the Communion class photos taken. On that day a troop of young boys and girls arrived to the school bedecked in suits, white dresses and shiny polished shoes. There was great excitement as we discussed what we had done for our Communion, where we had gone and, more importantly, how much money we had made.

After being initiated into all of this it was no wonder that religious fervour became part of our childhood. Mary was the epitome of holiness and the go-to role model for young girls. Every year as May approached my friends and I picked flowers for the May altars that we constructed in our bedrooms. There we prayed fervently to the Virgin, the most holy woman in the whole world, to be made pure and holy like her, even though we had no idea what this meant at all. The Rosary was part and parcel of our childhood. Every evening our mother would gather us together and we would recite the whole thing, kneeling on the floor. She took this very seriously while we avoided eye contact with each other in case we got a fit of the giggles. Every now and then she would get one of us to lead in one of the decades, keeping count as she listened, as we were prone to lop off a Hail Mary or two to hurry the whole thing along. As we got older it was the bane of our lives on the lovely summer evenings, but it was something she believed in and we had little choice in the matter.

In school I always did what I was told. You would too if you eyed the cane that stood in the corner of the classroom. In Junior Infants we were taught to write with a pencil, but when we moved up into First Class we had desks with fitted ink pots and we would labour for hours over perfect joined-up writing, while the nun patrolled the classroom, cane in hand, ready to pounce on anyone who didn't get it right. I can remember the humiliation of having to stand up and hold out my hand, and the sting of the cane across my palm, just because my joined-up writing wasn't up to scratch. In spite of this I don't remember school as being an awful place, partly because I was good and didn't rebel, and partly because I didn't find the lessons difficult. For anyone who struggled it was a different story though, as there was no recognition of learning difficulties, never mind any personal issues some of the children would have going on at home.

Most of us really feared our teachers, especially the nuns, and if we didn't fear them we had a healthy respect for them. When I was in Fifth Class the nun who was teaching us told me my sewing was disgraceful and she ordered me to go to the lay teacher in Fourth Class and show her how bad my work was. You have to wonder what the point of this was. To humiliate me in front of a younger class? Over a line of sewing. You really have to ask what made these women tick. Anyway, off I went, feeling very foolish and self-conscious. I stood outside the Fourth Class door for a while trying to pluck up the courage to go in and tell the teacher how bad my work was. She had been my teacher when I was in Fourth Class and, while she didn't take any nonsense, I can see now that she was one of those teachers who brought out the best in her students. Eventually I knocked on the door and opened it slightly. 'Yes,' she said, looking at me from above her glasses which were set on the bridge of her nose. 'I was told to show you my sewing,' I said. I didn't have the courage to tell her that I had been sent to show her how bad it was. She took it from me and examined it. 'Excellent,' she said, 'go around the class and show it to the girls. Very good work.' I couldn't believe my luck. To this day I don't know if she realised that I had been sent to her room as a punishment and she wasn't having it, or if she genuinely thought my sewing was great. I didn't care; I was just so relieved to have gotten off the hook.

In spite of the corporal punishment, which was part and parcel of home life as well as school life, I have good memories of my younger years. What stands out most for me when I reflect on that time is the imaginative play we engaged in. One of my youngest memories is of a pedal car I got for a Christmas present. I can remember our house being full, and pedalling this car as fast as I could around the legs of my adult relatives. In my mind I was driving a real car and they had better move out of the way. There was a great sense of festivity and togetherness as we all sat around the table for the meal. It is a memory that evokes happy times. Playing was an integral part of our lives and nothing was pre-organised. A knock on the door often signalled that our friends were there asking if we could come out to play. Once freed from any homework, household chores or mealtimes, which were part of our daily regime and strictly adhered to, we would disappear for hours at a time, hiking across fields or playing in makeshift huts. We could as easily be found in the shed in our back yard or swimming in the nearby river. The fields and hills were our frontiers, conquered through the power of fertile imaginations. Out there we lived the lives of cowboys, Indians, pirates, pioneers and innovators. A drain became a moat, and unless you have jumped drains as a kid you cannot imagine the excitement involved. This was life and death stuff, but we always managed to arrive home safely before it got dark, even though none of us possessed a watch. We spent hours playing hopscotch on the path outside our houses, or bringing our baby dolls for walks in their prams. We collected car registration numbers, something that baffles me when I think about it now, but we did it to see who could get the most reg numbers. If someone was lucky enough to get skates or a scooter for Christmas we careered down the hill near our house, with a look-out designated to shout 'Car!' whenever one was heard approaching. I had great aspirations of becoming a ballerina, courtesy of the *Judy* comic that I was allowed to buy every week, and impromptu ballet performances were often put on in the shed at the back of our house. My mother was an avid reader and we were enrolled in the local library from a young age. On the long summer evenings I loved playing rounders or football against the boys on the green next to the shop my father ran. The girls would egg each other on to beat the boys at this physical game. In the summer the older children led camping expeditions to Greenwood Forest, which seemed immense to us. There we would cook sausages in a tin can over a fire while the younger ones collected river water, which was then boiled to make tea. Then we would all go swimming in the river. We always seemed to be on the go, to be active.

There was a hole in the hedge at the bottom of our garden which we transformed into a secret hut, adorned with old strips of lino and tarpaulin to keep the rain out. This was our club. Membership was restricted to the friends of our choosing, and falling out with one another meant expulsion from the club until we made up and started over again. In spite of the freedom we were allowed our parents always knew where to look for us when the day was drawing in. When we eventually came home, after being called numerous times, a supper of cocoa and cream crackers or toast awaited us and we went to bed full of plans for future escapades. Looking back it seems so innocent, but our play encouraged imagination and socialisation and, while it may appear to have been risky, social media might be more of a danger to young people today. While our days were lived out within a structured regime of school, homework and religious and family duties, it is these hours of unfettered imaginative play that somehow stand out more in my memory than the duties of school or the Church.

While the wooden spoon may have been a cooking utensil it was used for more than cooking on many an occasion. We were punished for being bold, but sometimes it was hard to figure out what that meant. Answering back or being cheeky ensured you got a swipe of the spoon but sometimes the punishment was totally arbitrary, depending more on the mood of our mother than on anything we might have done. We were not unique in this regard. Most of my friends had the same complaints and even though we were subject to the vagaries of mood and corporal punishment, most of us did not feel we were being abused in any way. Some days you got a clatter for staying out in the rain and getting your clothes wet, while on others you got smacked for not going out, even though it was raining. My mother was a homemaker and a constant presence in our lives. She waved goodbye to us each morning on our way to school and was miraculously there at the window when we turned the corner to our house on the way home in the evenings. In the winter months when we arrived home from school, soaked and bedraggled, she would have a fire blazing and a hot drink ready for us. She knit all our sweaters, along with woolly balaclavas for the winter months. As we got older we would take the balaclavas off as we turned the corner in the morning and hide them in our pockets until we were almost home after school. Strictly religious, she made sure we attended every Church event that occurred, from the blessing of the throats on St Blaise's Day to the kissing of the cross on Good Friday. Anything that provided a leg up for entry to heaven and we were there. My father was the breadwinner; he brought home the money, was the voice of authority and never slapped us.

One look was enough. He loved music and had a great collection of old 78s. He would let us stand on his feet when we were younger and then dance around the floor carrying us along with him as he moved faster and faster. He brought us for Sunday afternoon drives into the countryside, where we had picnics and explored the surrounding hills and ditches. He would point out the different birds, plants and wildlife, which he loved to observe. He brought home sweets and chocolate and lanced my self-inflicted boils on an annual basis. He often brought us with him when he visited his friends in Donamona, near Drumraney. In the farmhouse there was a huge open fire with a large kettle that would swing back and forth on a crane and my father would sit there having tea. 'There's nothing like the tea that comes from that kettle,' he would remark. We were allowed to explore the surrounding fields and were introduced to the chickens, which we helped feed sometimes. We were warned to stay away from the huge black bull. He had a field all to himself and we were both terrified of and fascinated by him. My father, who liked game shooting, would sit talking with his friend about the up-and-coming pheasant season. He often brought us with him when he went clay pigeon shooting. I can remember one particular place where we picked what seemed like hundreds of bluebells and cowslips while he shot at clay pigeons with his friends. Once the pheasant shooting season began he would be up and gone at the crack of dawn and when we arrived home from school we would find pheasants hanging on the back of the scullery door. When we were younger my siblings and I would run past them in terror, their beady lifeless eyes following us. But we loved the coloured feathers and for part of the year pheasant was a staple of our diet.

When we were young my father worked on the railway and, sometimes, instead of being driven by my dad, we got the train to Galway. My mother would be greeted by the train driver and the conductor who knew my father and this made us feel very important. My father's goal was to become his own boss and eventually he left CIE to work as a salesman delivering sweets to shops around the county. If he wasn't travelling too far and we were on school holidays he would sometimes bring us with him in the sweet van, as we called it. This was far better than standing around while he shot dummy pheasants out of the sky. A van full of sweets was like an Aladdin's cave to us and the shopkeepers always offered us something when he stopped at the various shops. Sometimes he would let us sit in the front seat with him and, as we approached a bumpy road, he would rev up the engine so that we would get butterflies in our tummies. Later on he leased out a shop at the top of the road where we lived. Even though it was leased we always referred to it as our shop. This did not entitle us to special treatment though, and treats were reserved for the weekends. On Friday evenings when he closed up he would arrive home with chocolate or sweets, and after he had his tea and did his accounts he would stroll up to the pub at the top of the road (the same pub where we had held our hay-jumping competitions), have a couple of pints, and then come home with a Babycham for my mother. This was presented in a Babycham glass and we would admire the elegance of it and imagine having such a drink when we were grown up. For now, a bottle of TK red lemonade had to suffice. My father always closed the shop for an hour at lunchtime and some days he would collect us and bring us out to Coosan Point to go swimming. On one of those days I learned to swim without even realising it. I could see that he was watching me intently as I swam around. I had not noticed that the rubber ring I was using to keep myself afloat had in fact deflated. When he pointed this out to me, I was so thrilled to know that I could swim that I threw it away and began to swim around in the water. My father always instilled a sense of confidence in me. He was a social person, involved in various local events, and I can recall going to local fundraisers in St Mary's Hall, where he would be part of a committee for something or other, or advocating for the local Fine Gael party, of which he was a supporter. But he was at home most evenings, and between the domestic security my mother provided and the input of my father in our lives, we lived in a secure bubble and could never imagine any of this changing.

The highlight of our year was the annual trip to Galway. This was my mother's territory and all her family, except for her father who had died when she was a young child, still lived there. Every summer we packed our belongings into my father's car and hit the road to the west, where we stayed for five or six weeks. We never questioned the fact that he didn't stay with us on those long stretches away from home. He came down the odd Sunday to see us but other than that he remained back in Athlone, alone, except for whatever dogs he had at the time. Looking back now I wonder if he minded spending the summers on his own in Athlone. While we missed him when we were away, the excitement of being so near the seaside made up for this.

On hot summer days our playground was the Salthill promenade or the Grattan Beach, and I can still remember the excitement of our first trip of the year to the seaside. Whether we walked or rode the bus, another adventure in our eyes, the first sight of that blue water glittering in the sun had us giddy with excitement. Once we found a place on the sandy beach all we wanted to do was strip off, don our new swimsuits and race to the water. There was always a moment of apprehension, as if we had suddenly got something we were dying for but didn't know what to do with it. However, once we hit that water we never wanted to come out, and what began as a glorious day often ended in tears as we begged to be allowed to stay and my mother threatened us with all sorts if we didn't come out and get dressed. Teatime had to be adhered to and my grandmother was waiting at home for us. We would spend hours building sandcastles, which became more sophisticated as we got older, with moats and towers and sea water gathered to run through the canals we built. As well as the lure of the sea we had a group of friends with whom we were reacquainted each year, our Galway friends as we called them.

My grandmother's house was small and there was no indoor toilet. This was a great source of dread for us, especially if one of us needed to use the toilet after dark. My mother would have to accompany us and wait outside as we hurriedly did our business. There was an orchard next to my grandmother's house and the shadows cast by the tall trees gave an ominous air to her back yard, even though during the day we would dare one another to climb to the top of the highest trees and fill our pockets with juicy apples. We spent many happy hours climbing trees and being chased out of that orchard. The holiday was peppered with visits to Shantalla and Mervue, where our aunt and uncle lived, and we spent many a day exploring these areas. Trips to the Claddagh, the Spanish Arch and the docks to see the big ships were mixed with times of being indoors, especially if the weather turned bad. My granny had an old Singer sewing machine with a foot pedal, and while we were not allowed to touch this, she did let us set up shop in the back room using her box of buttons as money for purchases.

Galway was my mother's domain and when we went into town with her she would point out where O'Gorman's, the bookbinders, used to be. She had worked there before she married my father. A few years ago, when I was vising my aunt in Galway she showed me a photograph of a young woman by the name of Ethel Mannin. She was an author and my mother had met her in O'Gorman's. We laughed at the idea of only being six degrees away from a famous person. My mother had risen to the position of supervisor in O'Gorman's, a role that was unusual for a woman back then. Perhaps that is where she got her love of reading from. It was only when I was older that I realised how much she had given up in marrying my father and moving to Athlone. In Galway she had a life of independence and freedom in a vibrant city. In Athlone she was a wife and mother, totally dependent on my father. Apart from being away from him for such a long time, our summers were remarkable, and we didn't realise how lucky we were to have this time every summer. As we got older we were less inclined to want to spend so much time away from Athlone, from friends and the possibilities of boyfriends, but I treasure those times we spent in Galway as children.

One year when we came home from Galway my father surprised my mother with a new fireplace. He had arranged to have the old-fashioned range taken out and a new fireplace put in and he was excited to show her this. Unfortunately, in his haste to get the job done, he had forgotten to put in a back boiler. From now on the water would have to be heated with the immersion heater. Anyone familiar with this appliance in Irish homes will understand both the repercussions of this and my mother's reaction. She was not a bit impressed and my father's disappointment at her reception of his gift was palpable. For the first time I realised that there could be discord between my parents. Up to this we had never witnessed them quarrelling, but the atmosphere that day was really uncomfortable. Along with this discomfort came the realisation that we might be expected to take sides. I can still remember the sense of anger in the air as my father stormed out of the house. I found out later that he had gone straight up to his mother's house, which was nearby, where he had vented his anger and disappointment at the reaction to all the work he had done while we were off having a great time in Galway. Eventually they got over it but the moment remains locked in my memory. Anyone who remembers a childhood lived under the regime of the immersion heater will know what I mean when I say it was never fully forgotten.

My grandmother in Athlone was a formidable woman, not averse to getting involved in family issues. I have often wondered what she said to both of my parents about what happened that day. I know she would have felt sympathy for my father at the time and had her own opinion of my mother, which came out years later. But whatever transpired at this time, we were not privy to it. When she came to visit us she would park her car outside and sail up the path, her fur stole wrapped around her neck, her head held high. Appearances were very important to her and it made for a better life when everything was as it should be. She chain-smoked, lighting one cigarette from the butt of another while she chatted to my mother over endless cups of tea. When she left the house all the windows had to be opened. When we visited her house we usually stayed in the kitchen. She always had biscuits and other goodies in a press under the kitchen counter and she would offer us something nice from there. We played in her back garden which seemed enormous to us. I would not describe her as being particularly maternal but she always seemed pleased to see us. My grandfather was a quiet man. He would often be found weeding or doing other tasks in the garden. He allowed us to help him sometimes but always kept a strict eye on us in case we pulled out flowers by mistake. My grandparents would sit, one each side of the small kitchen table, drinking tea and chatting to my father. It was seldom that we were brought into the good sitting room, unless my aunt had arrived home from America for a visit. When I was a little older and she was home I would babysit for her. I was paid for this and she also gave me clothes, which seemed way too stylish for me at the time, but did make me feel a little more grown up. She didn't get home too often as travel to and from America was a big deal back then. My father brought us with him once when he was picking her up from the airport. On the way he stopped to let us see the planes taking off and landing. We were mesmerised. We had not yet been on a plane and were amazed to think that these huge vehicles could take off and fly through the air.

In comparison to my grandmother in Galway, my paternal grandmother always appeared very stylish. She would modulate her voice so that even when she was displeased, and there was no doubt that she was displeased, she still looked and sounded very sophisticated. My Galway grandmother's voice had a high-pitched cadence and always sounded shrill, so you were never sure if she was annoyed, excited or just making a general comment. She would sometimes call me Jacintia, something she found very amusing, though I didn't share her feelings on this. When my Athlone grandmother said my name it sounded as if she was treating me like an adult. She was a socialite and was involved in Fine Gael, the All-Ireland Drama Society and various other local groups. The two grandmothers were as different as chalk from cheese. I don't remember feeling particularly close to either of them, but this could be more to do with the attitude of children being seen and not heard that prevailed in those times. I can remember being very sad when my paternal grandfather died. I was violently sick the day of his funeral and cried hysterically. Maybe it was something to do with death and my reaction to it. Once, on a holiday in Galway, as I was getting ready to go to bed there was a film about the *Titanic* playing on the television. As the musicians played and the huge boat began to sink I burst into hysterical tears. I had no idea why. Maybe I was affected by the thought of so many people dying in the icy waters. My mother and grandmother gave out stink to me for being so melodramatic. When I started crying at my grandfather's funeral my aunt was very sympathetic and understood that even though I couldn't verbalise how I felt I was deeply affected by his death.

I don't know what the relationship between my father and his mother was like. Children were not allowed to witness that sort of emotion back then, but as it was to her that he turned after the fireplace debacle he must have felt that he could talk to her. On the day of my grandfather's funeral my aunt seemed comfortable talking about how I felt. That day was, however, a harbinger of what was to come, a slight crack that could be papered over, even ignored, but there all the same. Up to this our lives had been uncomplicated, easy-going and unrestricted on the whole. We were protected from the outside world, unaware of the problems that beset many of the families whose homes and gardens we played in. We lived in a cosy bubble of safety. Everything we needed was provided and we were rigorously shielded from the darker aspects of society and from anything deemed inappropriate for our young eyes and ears. The term 'unmarried mother' would have meant nothing to me, but then again, any mention of sex was strictly prohibited, even as we grew older. I loved my mother, idolised my father and thought my life was perfect. Little did I realise the changes that would impact my family and myself personally by the time I was heading into my teens.

I cannot write about Bessborough House without writing about my father. When I was eleven years of age something happened that changed the trajectory of my life and that of my family forever. My father, who had been a constant figure in my life, began an affair with a woman who lived nearby. Today, this may not seem like such a big deal, but in 1960s Ireland it was not a common occurrence, or, if it was, it was not conducted openly. The family unit was sacrosanct and this event had a domino effect on all our lives. I felt that I was catapulted out of the safe cocoon of childhood and into the world of adult drama without any preparation. The man who had held my hand throughout my young life, introduced me to the wildlife of the countryside, taught me to swim and been protector and provider of safety was now the very one who threatened the existence of my safe environment. One night in July 1969, just three months before my twelfth birthday, something happened that brought us face to face with the reality of the situation.

The man turned the key stealthily in the lock, quietly opening the door and waiting for a moment to see if anyone had heard him come in. To his surprise he heard murmured voices coming from the front room of the house. He quietly closed the door and waited for a few minutes, unsure of what to do next. Should he just creep up the stairs and slip into bed, or should he investigate. 'Who could be up at this hour?' he wondered to himself. His wife was usually in bed early and his children were too young to be up at this time. It was almost three in the morning, for God's sake! Up to now he had managed to sneak home at all hours and no one had said anything. But he could not ignore the noises coming from the front room. 'This is my house', he thought, as he turned the handle and opened the door. He was taken aback to find his wife and children glued to the small black-and-white television set, which relayed the grainy image of Neil Armstrong as he took his first step on the moon. 'One small step for man, one giant leap for mankind', the astronaut said, as he took the historic step. As his wife and family turned to look at him, the man thought of the giant reper-cussions the small, almost silent turn of his key in the door that morning had wrought for his family.

I like to imagine what went through my father's mind that morning when he opened the door and saw all of us sitting up to watch Neil Armstrong's historic walk on the moon. I like to imagine his expression of surprise and guilt. But in reality memories can be misleading and what I have projected onto that morning is what I think of now. I do remember his absence at this historic event, how we all sat silently when we heard the key turn in the door, knowing who it was but saying nothing. I remember how we all turned to face him, then turned back to look at the screen, the images there appearing more important than his appearance at that hour of the morning. Somewhere deep inside me I recognised that what was unfolding in our front room was more important than any moon walk, and that we could no longer hide behind silence. I didn't fully understand the ramifications of that night, but just three months off my twelfth birthday I felt as if I had lost my father in some way. But I swallowed this realisation and turned around like the rest of the family to watch an image coming from far away. This seemed like the safest option at the time and while that night was never fully forgotten, like the day of the fireplace debacle, it was put away and not mentioned again.

2

He's Leaving

'Funny how you lose sight of some things and memory others.'
— Toni Morrison, *Beloved*

How do you sift through the memories and images of the past when it's so hard to pin them down? When it's so difficult to recall the exact time frame or chronology of the events? I know what happened in my life between the ages of twelve and sixteen but it's difficult to put it all together, to chart the path between events, even though the images and feelings that accompany that time still wrap themselves around me, trailing wisps of joy and sorrow, horror and incredulity. Memories of myself in my new school uniform when I started secondary school evoke a feeling of hope, of potential, of promises to come. Three years later everything had changed. It was as if I had been thrust outside of the orbit of everything I knew and found myself living a life I had never imagined. A lifetime of experiences would be crammed into a few short years, expunging the wonderful childhood memories that preceded that time and clearing the way for chaos, hurt and pain. I write about these memories as I picture them, even if the timeline seems confusing at times. I write about them with the feelings they evoke in me, even to this day. I take them out and look at them, not to apportion blame to myself or anyone else, but to help me to understand how quickly life can change and how one decision can impact not just on one life, but on the future lives of all involved.

The first inkling that life wasn't all roses and sunshine occurred the day I witnessed the tension between my parents during the fireplace debacle. But that day was soon set aside as we got on with our lives. When my grandfather was diagnosed with cancer we were considered too young to be told the details, but looking back it seems as if his illness was swift and terrible. We knew he was in a hospital called St Luke's, in Dublin, but we didn't realise the significance of this at the time. He died in September 1968, just a month before my eleventh birthday. I remember him as a quiet, unassuming gentleman. He allowed us to help while he weeded the garden or quietly asked how we were doing while slipping some loose change into our waiting hands. I was too young to realise the grief my grandmother was feeling or what the loss of his presence would mean to my father, his only son. On the day of his funeral my aunt from America comforted me when I got upset, taking time out from her own grief to reassure me that I would be okay. She allowed me articulate my feelings and told me they were natural. My grandfather's death coincided with a time when things would begin to change for our family.

When I look back now it is hard to reconcile that young girl with the girl who travelled to Bessborough House just four short years later, but on that day such an idea was inconceivable. Losing our grandfather was sad, but we had little time to think of it as another crisis hit our family soon afterwards. Almost immediately after my grandfather's death my father became seriously ill. He had noticed a lump on his neck on the day of his father's funeral, and as cancer was the foremost thought in his mind he went to see his doctor as soon as he could. Within a week he too found himself in St Luke's, where he was diagnosed with thyroid cancer. This was the first time we realised death could reach out its hand to one of our parents and even though we didn't know all the details of what he was going through, we had just seen our grandfather, who had been in the same hospital with the same illness, buried. So it didn't take too much for us to feel scared about what was happening with our father. Over the following months he had a number of hospital stays, culminating in a 'make or break' operation that would determine whether the disease had been eliminated or not. On the morning of this operation, early in 1969, he was prayed for in the school assembly, and that alone said all that was needed about the enormity of the situation. Personal prayers during assembly only happened when there was something serious going on. The day he arrived home after his last operation was a very exciting one for us. We watched through the window for his car to pull up and when it did we rushed out through the front door, unable to contain ourselves. But when we saw his face we stopped abruptly. He didn't look like our father. His face was lopsided from the surgery and he didn't look like himself. He was our father, but he didn't look like our father. We could see his disappointment at our hesitation. He had been looking forward to seeing us, just as much as we had been looking forward to seeing him again. When we ran to him he hugged us tightly, and there he was, the father we had always known. It felt strange, yet familiar, almost as if we were getting to know him again even though he was such a permanent fixture in our lives. We did get him back, this time, but he was never really the same after that, as if his leaving was always inevitable. He slept in the spare room. We were told it was because the pain he experienced was so severe that it would wake him up and he couldn't get back to sleep again. My mother had the room adorned with religious icons to protect and comfort him, but maybe his mind was on comfort of another kind. Things were changing, and it wasn't just my father's illness that prompted that change. It was in June 1969 that he crept stealthily into the house in the early hours of the morning during the historic moon landing, the same year that he had his final surgery, the year that would see him regain his health, the year that the truth was revealed about his affair. In a short space of time we had lost our grandfather and almost lost our father to cancer. The harsh truth was that even though he was still here we had already lost him. I know these events occurred, but they sometimes seem difficult to comprehend, as if the memories are wrong in my mind in some way. How could so much change so quickly?

There is one happy memory I have that replays itself in my mind and that is the memory of the last birthday present I received from both of my parents. I can't remember which birthday it was but I can see the three of us, standing in front of the old wireless that was set on top of a table in the corner of the kitchen. A record player built into the wireless played LPs and EPs, and as they wished me a happy birthday they presented me with the *Sound of Music* soundtrack and a beautiful leather shoulder bag. The presents seem a little grown up for an eleven-year-old, but by the time of my twelfth birthday in October 1969 my father was spending his evenings with another woman, so it's hard to believe this happened on that later birthday. Is the image of us standing together around the wireless something I like to remember, something viewed through rose-tinted glasses? I can't be sure of the exact dates, but I can remember the feelings that surrounded that day. I was delighted with my presents, slightly disappointed with the music selection, as Julie Andrews was not someone I would have listened to at that time, but delighted all the same. I was beginning to develop an interest in pop music and I would have preferred music from the Top Ten. 'Sugar Sugar' from the Archies, or 'Good Morning Starshine' by Oliver would have been preferable. But I hugged my father and thanked him. I knew the music part of the gift came from him. He was an avid music fan and had a great collection of LPs, ranging from opera to jazz and popular music. I can also remember the sense of smug satisfaction I felt when I put the bag over my shoulder. It was obviously an expensive one, made of brown leather with leather tassels at the end. I was thrilled with it, though there was also a slight feeling of apprehension that was alleviated only when my friends gave their seal of approval to the gift. It's strange to remember the feelings with such precision but not the timeline. Even if the date eludes me the accompanying images and feelings are very real and I can still see us, standing in front of that old wireless as we played the LP. It's the first time I can remember pretending to love a present even though I didn't really, and I can remember the feeling of wearing the shoulder bag as I left the house to show it to my friends. There is another memory from around this time, which causes even more confusion, one where my parents wear very different expressions, but that is for later in the story. It's a memory I and my siblings have ruminated on, with different versions and different timelines. Just as the memory of the birthday gifts conjures up very real feelings of happiness and connection, this memory also conjures up strong feelings, but these are of shock, anger, fear and abandonment.

I was in secondary school when we were told of my father's affair. There was enough underlying tension in the home at this time to warn us that something bad was happening, but because it wasn't spoken about everything had the appearance of being the same. Moving from primary to secondary school is enough in itself to keep anyone occupied, never mind trying to figure out what is happening at home. The enormity of such a move cannot be underestimated. In the final year of primary school I can remember the importance of being in the top class and how the new girls in Second Class would look up to us Sixth Classers. That is unless, of course, one of us was an older sister and was just sneered at. In the hierarchy that prevails in every school system the final year of school is definitely the place to be. By then you have firmly established yourself both academically and socially. You know the ropes, the best places to hide, the teachers you have to apply yourself for and the ones you can wrap around your little finger. In short, you have finally figured out what they expect from you, and as long as you give them what they expect life is plain sailing. The major worries in Sixth Class were preparing for Confirmation and the challenge of moving to secondary school. My Confirmation was another family affair. My clothes were bought from the local drapery, a classic dress-and-coat outfit which, though very grown up, was not what I would have picked given my own choice. But my mother oversaw all domestic elements of life and clothing us was one of her duties. She had the last word on the outfit, so, duly presented in my yellow dress and coat, my patent shoes and long white socks, I agreed to receive all the wonderful gifts the Holy Ghost had to offer without really thinking through what any of this meant. In roughly three years I would be the mother of a child and, as I write this, I have mixed emotions of fear and sadness for the young girl I was then. Nothing could have prepared me for what was to come, but on my Confirmation day I didn't think of things like unmarried mothers or mother and baby homes. Such things were so far off my radar that I wouldn't have considered them. After the service we visited my grandmother and my aunts where my outfit was admired and I collected my Confirmation money. Then my father brought us out to his friends in Donamona, where more money was collected and photos were taken in the farmyard. I remember that day as a good one, even though things were on the cusp of change for my family. As usual we spent that summer in Galway. When we returned I moved into another phase of my life. Now I would be one of the new girls, back to the bottom of the ladder in the pecking order.

Secondary school brought its own challenges. Along with having to deal with different subjects, different teachers and a busy timetable, there was the issue of fitting in and finding my place in this world. My coping mechanism when facing change of any kind was to imagine different scenarios that might occur. How would I speak to the different teachers? How would I react to different situations? I had an intense fear of being caught on the back foot, seeming unprepared, or, worse still, being perceived as stupid. It was important to me to be prepared, in my head at least. That is why impromptu exams would cause me to freeze, and even the thought of them can elicit this reaction to this day. Maybe that is one of the reasons I couldn't cope with the enormous change in our family circumstances when it finally materialised. If I thought secondary school was going to be the big change in my life I was in for a lot of future shocks. As well as having to deal with this new academic and social world, there were the physical changes occurring in my body and the hormonal changes in my moods to figure out. Entering adolescence is not easy. Some of the new subjects were interesting but it took time to get used to the different teaching styles of the various teachers and the concept of moving classrooms for different subjects. The worry of making it in time to a different classroom caused a lot of anxiety until we settled in. I knew some of my classmates as they had been in the same primary school as me but there were new people to get to know. Then there was the intimidation of the Sixth Years. Not that any of them ever lowered themselves to intimidate us First Years, but even being around them was intimidating. They were like adult women to us and seemed so grown up and so confident. Of course, in my later life I realised that this was not true, but it appeared so at the time. In spite of all the strange new experiences I felt I was finding my feet. I had begun to make new friends and did well at some of the subjects, but it was a time of upheaval, and along with the new-found academic maturity came issues of body image (what do I look like in this awful maroon uniform?), popularity and the pull of peer groups. Is it better to do well or to fit in? Unfortunately, the answer to this question often doesn't become clear until an exam year looms, and by then it can be too late. For me there was the realisation that while I might not be a genius I had the ability to do well in school. However, the unravelling of our home life would interrupt all of this.

Confirmation day had come and gone, Neil Armstrong had taken his heroic first step on alien ground; my father was not my father any more. The outstanding memory of that time, the one that causes so much confusion, the one that hovers around the edges of the page even as I write this is the memory of the night my mother took us out of bed and brought us downstairs to witness my father's leaving. Or was it the night he left? It is such a fractured memory, so full of pain, anger, loss and abandonment, that sometimes it is hard to recall it fully even though it is etched on my brain. Long before this night I had begun to suspect that my father was having an affair. It was the only thing that made sense of the way he had changed. He was out much more in the evenings and he was particularly friendly with this one woman who used to deliver goods to our shop. Though he was naturally affable and chatted to everyone, he spent more time with her, often following her out as she was leaving and spending what seemed like ages chatting to her outside her van. Now that I was in secondary school conversation between groups of girls often focused on boyfriends and on sex. I didn't have a boyfriend yet but I knew that adult men and women had sex. It's hard to relate this to your own parents, but there had to be some reason for the tension between my parents. There was definitely something wrong. One day I plucked up the courage to ask my mother if she thought my father was having an affair, but that was the wrong question to ask her and I was probably the wrong person to ask it. She shut down that conversation very quickly. Maybe I was wrong. Surely he would never do anything like that? Eventually, though, what I had suspected began to become more obvious as he stopped hiding where he was spending his evenings. What made it more obvious was that this woman's house could be seen plainly from my parents' bedroom and we often witnessed him pulling up to the front of her house when we were hanging out with friends. This brings me back again to that memory that I keep avoiding, as if reliving every other one will negate it. My siblings and I have different versions of what happened that night. My memory is of our mother waking us up and telling us to come downstairs. When we walked, bleary-eyed, into the living room, my father was slumped in one of the armchairs. He looked tired and deflated, while my mother seemed agitated. In hindsight she must have been terrified to do such a thing. We were half asleep, and what was happening was so outside of the norm for us that it was hard to figure out what was going on. I remember this night through the eyes of my younger self. I cannot imagine what it was like for either of them. My father had his coat on as if he was ready to leave or had just come in.

'Your father is having an affair,' our mother said. 'He's going to leave us and go off with her.'

He remained silent with his head lowered. We knew who 'her' was, but it had never entered my mind that he would actually leave. All I could see was the end of everything familiar, everything safe, everything I had ever known. We were in strange territory now. I remember looking from one of them to the other and then turning on my heel and going back to bed. I lay facing the wall and something shut down deep inside me, something that would take years to slowly open up again. In my memory, some time later he came up to our room and told me how sorry he was and he said goodbye. I determined there and then that I would never let anyone or anything hurt me like that again. I would never trust anyone again. This was total and absolute dissociation, but back then it was a coping method that offered protection. I would be well into my 30s before I began slowly to unfurl that closed-up part of me.

The strange thing about this particular memory is that when I discussed it with one of my siblings she had a different memory of that night. Yes, our mother did wake us up and ask us to come downstairs. Yes, my father was sitting in the armchair, his overcoat on as if he had come in from somewhere or was preparing to leave. But in my sister's memory the reason my mother brought us downstairs was to tell us that he was having an affair, not that he was leaving. As far as she can remember he did not leave for at least another two years. I find it difficult to reconcile my memory with hers. We knew he was seeing someone before he left, we even knew who it was, and the timeline of the events she remembered didn't add up for me. Memories are indeed strange entities, and trauma renders them stranger still. While we have both agreed to disagree on the timeline, the reality is that one night we were all brought downstairs to witness my father's failings. We had front row seats to the disintegration of their marriage. I'm not sure what we were expected to do about it. Would he stay if we begged him? Could we have stopped him? Was it right that we were pulled into this? Regardless of the difference in the details we remember, there is no doubting the strength of emotion that reliving this memory brings up. The trauma of that night is etched so deeply within us that neither of us can accurately place the dates and times in their correct order, as if the memories are still rippling in the aftershock of some seismic event. And that was what it felt like. It was as if the earth shifted on its axis and everything that we had believed to be secure – the safety, the love, the familiarity – had all disappeared down a bottomless hole of betrayal and abandonment. The events of that night caused each of us to remember and react in different ways, but the feelings were very similar.

That was the night I truly lost my father and, as a result, lost part of myself also. It was only later that I found out the affair had begun in 1969, so maybe my sister's recollection is the truer one. The uneasy, unrecognised atmosphere in the home had not been imagined. I often wonder if he had met this woman even earlier, when he was sick, or if the impact of his brush with death had affected the decisions he made at this time. I am sure that losing his father and coming so close to death himself so soon afterwards must have caused him to re-evaluate his life. While extramarital affairs may be acknowledged more openly today, it doesn't take away from the reality of the damage they can inflict on everyone involved, particularly if they are not handled well by the parents. Access to divorce and less control by the Church does not take away from the emotional and psychological damage that can be wrought in these situations. The impact of this on a family, especially on the children, is often underestimated. What was happening in my parent's relationship destroyed the safe world we lived in and it seemed the ground under our feet was suddenly gone, leaving a gaping chasm that threatened to swallow us up. That the affair was so open and was common knowledge in our close-knit community was also devastating and embarrassing. Everyone knew, long before I had my first suspicions. While we were getting on with our lives, people were talking. Time has blurred the sequence of events for me, though it has never blurred the strength of the feelings it left me with or my distrust of relationships.

In the time leading up to his final leaving we tried various ways to stop the inevitable, but the silly immature trips we made to this woman's house didn't change anything. We were children and reacted in a childish way, throwing muck at her washing, trying to let the air out of his tyres, calling them names. Once I even threw an empty milk bottle at him. It sailed over his head because he happened to stoop down just as I threw it. He couldn't believe what I had done. I couldn't either and I knew I had better get out of there quickly. He closed the shop and chased me up to the house where I had hidden in the bathroom. My mother had to contain him. It was an attempt on my part both to punish him and try to stop him, an attempt to get his full attention, to maybe make him rethink what he was about to do, and what he was about to lose. But it was futile. I was angry with my mother also, frustrated that from where I was sitting she wasn't making any effort to stop things or fighting to keep the family together. Again, it was only when I was older that I realised how powerless she must have felt. She was a widow when she met my father. Her husband had died suddenly when they were on honeymoon. How awful it must have been to have to go back home and work through that, get her life together and eventually marry again, only to have it all fall apart in front of her eyes. It almost broke her. I wasn't thinking of any of that on the day I threw the empty milk bottle at my father. I was a seething mass of contradictions. I hated him, I loved him, I wanted him to go, I wanted him to stay. I wanted everything back to the way it was, yet somehow I knew this would never happen, it would never be the same again.

When we were younger, long after my father had left CIE, he would sometimes travel up to Dublin on business trips. He told us it was something to do with his pension. One day he asked me if I would like to go up with him. I was very excited as it would mean I would get to spend a whole day with him. I could sit in the front seat of the car as there were only the two of us. There would be none of the usual fighting over who would sit in the front and who would sit in the back. I waved goodbye to my mother and we headed for Dublin. I couldn't believe it when he stopped the car and picked his girlfriend up. What should I do? Demand to be brought home? That is probably what one of my siblings would have done. But I was tongue-tied. I didn't know how to react and sat quietly in the back while they both tried to make small talk with me. It was awful. And what had promised to be a great adventure was now a great betrayal. I ask myself now, 'What was he thinking in doing this? What reaction did he expect from me?' To rub salt into the wound he insisted that I hold her hand when crossing the road on the quays. I couldn't wait for the day to be over. They stopped for something to eat on the way home and what would have been a real treat was now such a let-down. To cap it all I had to go home and tell my mother, even though I was asked not to. I couldn't do that to her. All in all, the handling of the whole situation was a lesson in how not to have an affair and how not to damage your children through your own actions. Later in my life, when I learned how easy it was to fail others as an adult, I was less judgemental of my parents, particularly of my father, but it is a memory that will never disappear. On another occasion I joined my father for a Sunday afternoon walk. He probably wanted some time alone but I asked if I could go with him. As we walked along the old Coosan Road, he had his hands in his coat pockets. It was a cold day and he had forgotten to bring his gloves. I slipped my hand into his, thinking that if I held on tightly enough he would stay with us. But the die was cast, and one morning when we came down for breakfast he was gone. He had left in the night and he was not coming back. We were alone with each other, with all that that entailed. I often wondered if it was difficult for him to leave. What would drive someone who had been such a good husband and father to leave his family behind, leave all he had worked for and start a new life? I wish both of my parents had handled things differently. I wish most of all that we had not become the casualties of the adult war, tossed between both of them, swinging on the pendulum of blame and wondering where the hell we fitted into the picture.

It was around this time that I met the boy would become my boyfriend, the boy who would feature so prominently in my life. I'm not sure whether to refer to him as a boy or a man as he was older than me. I don't remember when I first saw him, or became aware of him as someone I was attracted to. We lived in the same terrace and one of my friends lived across the road from his house but he would have been well off my radar because of the age difference. Everyone knew everyone in the town back then and it was inevitable that we would hang around with the same people eventually. I was fourteen when we met and he was twenty-one. He was just one of the lads as far as I was concerned until I realised that there was an attraction there on my side. He was good-looking and cocky and I would have felt totally out of my depth if he even spoke to me, but without my realising it he suddenly seemed to be everywhere I was. Maybe somewhere in my subconscious I was already trying to replace the most important male figure in my life. My father was always someone I could depend on. He was always there to protect me. Maybe I was trying to replicate that. Once, when cycling down a rocky lane, the very lane that we would creep down just a few years later in order to throw the muck at her washing, I hit a rock and flew over the handlebars of my bike. Before I knew what was happening, my father was there. Someone had told him of my accident and he had closed the shop immediately to look after me. On another occasion, when I was allowed to go to my first disco, a boy I knew asked if he could walk me home. These were childish events, everyone walked to the venue and there were no lifts or chaperones like today. We all walked home together as well. I was very shy when I was younger, and while some of my friends already had boyfriends,

or boys who were interested in them, I always felt a bit out of my depth
about the idea of a boyfriend. It would be great to have one, but I wouldn't
know how to be around a boy. We were excited about the night and left our
respective homes with the usual warnings. 'Make sure you're home before
midnight.' 'Be careful.' 'Stay together, and come home together.' Once
there and over the initial shyness we had fun, dancing and chatting to boys
we knew from school or from the town, and giggling together in groups.
To my surprise a boy did ask to walk me home. He was someone I would
have thought of as more mature than me and I was trying to act cool. On
the way home he tried to hold my hand. I tentatively took hold of his but
was somewhat distracted by a car that was driving very slowly behind us and
seemed to be following us. Imagine my horror when I realised it was my
father, who was keeping a beady eye on this boy and making sure nothing
unseemly happened. I quickly took my hand away and when we got to my
gate I said a hurried goodbye and ran inside. When my father arrived in
behind me I was interrogated about who this boy was and how I knew him,
and I was reminded that I was too young to be going with boys. If only that
guardianship had been around in the later years, my life might have turned
out very differently. When my father left that safety net disappeared with
him and we all went a bit wild.

It seems as if one day myself and this older boy were strangers to each
other and the next we were inseparable. I couldn't believe that he had
chosen me. He could have had his pick of any girl, girls better-looking than
me, older, cooler. But he had chosen me and I was crazy about him. We
began to spend more and more time together. We were in love, and swore
that nothing would ever separate us. Now I question if what I thought of
as love was instead a deep need on my part for some sort of connection,
some sort of healing, some sort of resolution of my family situation. I have
asked my siblings if they can remember when I started going out with
him, but they are not really sure. My sister says it is as if he was always
there. But obviously he wasn't there when I was eleven, or twelve. I can
only remember meeting him when I was in secondary school and moving
into my teenage years, when I was probably around fourteen. I went into
Bessborough Mother and Baby home when I was fifteen so I must have
met him when I was just about fourteen. I was definitely going out with
him when I was doing my Intermediate Certificate exam in 1971. I know

this because halfway through my Inter Cert mocks I ran away with him to England.

One Saturday morning, I left my house dressed in my sports culottes, because they looked better than my normal school skirt, and instead of going to the school sports day, where I had told my mother I was going, we boarded a train and then a boat and headed to London. I was going to find my father and introduce my boyfriend to him. What was I thinking? That my father would welcome us both with open arms, give us work and let us live with him? Whatever crazy ideas were in my head they were dispelled very quickly when I saw the expression on my father's face the day we arrived in the pub he managed in London. My boyfriend was given short shrift and I was allowed to stay with my father for one week, kept on a short leash, and then sent home. I knew I was in the way. He was trying to start a new life and there was no room for me in it. I didn't realise it at the time but I was still desperately trying to drag him back to his old life. Always getting in the way, and it wouldn't be the last time either. I asked if he would buy a plane ticket for my boyfriend, but there was no way he was doing that. Instead he warned me to keep away from him, but I knew he wasn't going to do anything about this as his new life was more important to him. I was deposited on the plane and met at Dublin Airport by my uncle, who drove me back to Athlone. I remember clearly my aunt saying to my mother, 'Don't give out to her. Run her a bath and let her settle in.' I think she realised how hurt and confused I was after the separation of my parents. To my surprise that is exactly what my mother did. Don't underestimate what this meant in the time of the immersion heater! I went back to school and continued to study for my Intermediate Certificate exam even though I had missed half my mocks. It took my boyfriend longer to get the money together to get home. The day he finally arrived back in Athlone I was on my way down to my friend's house when I spotted his distinctive walk as he came over the hill, the same hill we used to roller skate and scooter down when we were kids. I ran up to him and he grabbed me and swung me around. 'How is my little cow?' he said, and I could feel the hurt and disappointment run through me. Nobody had ever called me a cow before, and while he insisted it was a term of endearment, to me it sounded like a term used to insult someone. Later I put it down to something they might have said in London, maybe a local saying, but it was the first time I had really felt disappointed and out of my depth in the relationship.

I had persuaded my mother to let me leave school after my Inter Cert exam. While it was true that the extra money would help I didn't really want to stay in school. I wanted to be an adult, to earn my own money, buy my own clothes and go out when I wanted. I wanted to spend time with my boyfriend and get married as soon as I was old enough. We talked about it all the time, what kind of house we would have, how many children we would have. We were like kids playing make-believe. I would prove that it could be done, families could stay together. I would do it right, not like them. I was always trying to recreate the family I had lost. It sounds ludicrous now, but at fourteen years of age, while my friends were making plans to go on to do their Leaving Certificate, maybe travel, or get a good job in the Civil Service, which was the apex of achievement for young women at this time, I wanted to be a wife, a mother, a fixer of the past. Even though this was the early 1970s and the women's movement was beginning in America and England, in a suburban town in Midlands Ireland at this time there wasn't much choice for young women. Marriage, the Church or the Civil Service were seen as great prospects. I was too young to be aware of what was going on politically in the rest of the world. All I wanted to do was go out at the weekends, plan the house we would have when we got married and reconstruct the fractured home of my childhood. Back then I thought I was in love and had met my soulmate. When we had been in England, before I brought him to meet my father, we had both looked for work. I had gone for an interview with Marks & Spencer and had been offered a job, just like that. That was back in the day when you could work at fourteen. If I had taken it and if he had got a job we were planning on making a life there for ourselves. Maybe we could have settled there. I wonder how long that would have lasted. My father would never have allowed it though, or my mother. I didn't think of how worried she must have been when I just disappeared that day. I didn't stop to think about how she had gone through so much and then had to contend with a runaway daughter. I was totally self-absorbed and on a very self-destructive path.

The memories I share from that time are the important ones, the ones that make me think back and take stock. Perhaps the most traumatic was the day I took an overdose of tablets. My mother had decided that I should live with my grandmother in Athlone for a while. For the life of me I can't remember what reason she gave for this but I'm sure she was at her wits' end trying to figure out what to do with me. My grandmother, who never came across as a maternal figure in my life, must have also seen how troubled I was and wanted to help. To this day I cannot articulate what was going on in my head, but for some reason one day I decided to take all the tablets that were in my grandmother's medicine cabinet. I didn't even check to see what they were for. I just downed them all and then went off to meet my boyfriend. I don't believe that I wanted to die but I was crying out to be heard or understood in some way. I was accused afterwards of being an attention-seeker, but now I know that when someone goes that far to seek attention there is a problem that needs to be identified and the person needs help. I couldn't figure out how I felt back then so I don't know how I expected anyone else to. It was as if we were just supposed to get on with our lives and forget that our father had left even though our whole lives were in turmoil. Maybe I thought my father would come home if I almost died. After I took the tablets I went to meet my boyfriend and we went to a local bar for a drink. Halfway through the drink I told him what I had done. At first he didn't believe me, but when he realised I was telling the truth he tried to bring me to the local hospital, which was within walking distance. Halfway there I began to stumble and couldn't walk or talk properly. He stopped a passing car and got them to drive me the rest of the way. They got me inside and pumped my stomach. They told me afterwards that if I had not gotten there when I did it would have been too late. My mother couldn't understand why I would do this to her. My boyfriend couldn't understand why I would do this to him. No one attempted to understand why a young girl would do something so drastic. My boyfriend and my mother had never been overly friendly; she didn't approve of him. But now they were united in their disappointment with me and their unanimous belief that I was just plain selfish. I couldn't understand why I had done this either, and I couldn't explain how I felt, but it was as if I was constantly looking for someone to step in and change things or control them. I didn't have the words to explain how I felt, not even to myself.

When I look back now it's as if I was constantly treading water, a milli-second away from being drowned. I was in an adult relationship although I was still a child, sexually active without being sexually aware. I had no idea what intimacy was, never mind sexual intimacy. I was not using any protection, never giving a thought to getting pregnant and blindly believing that this would never happen to me. I believed love would keep me safe without having any notion of what love was or what it entailed. When I did eventually become pregnant I didn't even know it. I was fifteen and every good thing that I experienced in the first decade of my life was negated, totally undone. And I was still shut down, closed off to myself and to the feelings of others. I thought I could control my life, even though I was still a child in many ways. How I found out I was pregnant is a story in itself, one that could only have happened in twentieth-century Ireland.

3

The Visitation

'The angel of the Lord declared unto Mary …'

– The Angelus

It was not unusual to have one of the local priests arrive at the front door without notice. I was sitting at the large dining-room table at our front window when I saw him striding up the front path. I shouted to my mother, presuming he was calling to see her.

'Mam, it's the priest. He's at the front door.'

At that time priests had the divine right to call to any house unannounced. Sometimes they arrived on their own, sometimes in pairs and sometimes, if there was a mission, three of them could rock up. Crowding into the room they asked questions a guard wouldn't dream of asking. Questions regarding faith, family, attendance at Mass and religious observances. 'Where were you between the hours of ten and eleven last Sunday?' 'I was at Mass, your worship'. Honestly, it was like being interrogated. It didn't matter what time of the day it was, how busy the woman of the house was; whether she was arm deep in suds from the twin tub, or in the middle of cooking dinner. Everything was put to one side and they were invited in and offered tea. When questions were asked answers were expected. It was the confession box and the priest's house visits that gave the clergy access to information about their parishioners. They were a nosy lot. So, when I saw him, my first reaction was to call my mother and disappear upstairs. She could look after him. I and a lot of my friends were at the stage of questioning the relevance of this intrusion in our daily lives. I mean, who did they think they were, and why did my mother always kowtow to them, giving them a reverence they did not deserve? There was a scullery off the dining/living area of our house and she had been busy working there. She quickly washed her hands and came out to greet him. I waited to say the obligatory hellos, then began to move towards the stairs. To my surprise she turned to me and said, 'He's here to see you.' My heart sank as I tried to figure out what he could possibly want with me. The only reason I could come up with was that my family hated me seeing this older boy and they had asked him to have a word to me about it.

'Stop seeing him.'

'He's too old for you.'

'This will all end in tears.'

'Think of your family.'

I had heard it all before so I put on my best poker face and waited for the lecture. As there was nowhere we could talk, unless we or the rest of my family went into the scullery, my mother decided that they would all wait upstairs while we had our chat. I could hear them troop into her bedroom and I didn't miss the looks of curiosity and annoyance that were fired at me as they left the room. They would be stuck upstairs with her for however long this chat took.

Fair enough, I had gone off the rails a bit when my father left home. I neatly sidestepped the trauma of his leaving by hanging out with my boyfriend and my friends, drinking, smoking hash and going out at the weekends. But I also helped out as much as I could at home and in the shop that he had also abandoned and which we were losing more control of each day. None of us had any idea how to run a business. My mother, who had been so independent as a young woman, was at a loss as to what to do when it came to the running of the shop. She had been the homemaker, my father the breadwinner. That was the way it was. Now he was gone and we were left with the debris. She was reeling after he left, and much as we tried to help we were too young to understand the dynamics of the retail industry. I did want to help but I couldn't see the bigger picture, none of us could. We were too young and we didn't know what kind of future was waiting for us or what else could go wrong. We couldn't see any further than getting through each day. Better to wear my impenetrable self-protective shield, the one that stopped me getting hurt again, and just get on with it. As long as we could keep going and nothing else happened we would be okay. We had always had a good life, with everything we needed provided for. But our father had left us with nothing, except a pile of debts. There was no income and no way to pay off these debts, except keep the shop open, and that wasn't going so well. Overnight life changed from one of perceived privilege to one of lack. One day there was a knock at the door and a couple of men informed us that they were from a debt collection agency. They were there to search the house for anything that would make up for the debts my father owed. My mother, who had never owed a penny in her life, must have been mortified. They wanted to take a set of encyclopaedias that my father had purchased when we were younger and the cash register from the shop. The enormity of what was happening didn't fully sink in with me at the time. Yes, it was embarrassing and it fuelled an anger towards my father that would take years to calm down, but it is only as an adult that I can even begin to imagine what my mother must have suffered during all of this. His leaving affected us in so many ways, emotionally, psychologically, financially. It felt at the time that we were left without any protection in an unfamiliar world. We had to come up with our own strategies now, and the coping mechanisms of a fourteen-year-old are not always the healthiest. Helping in the house and shop and trying to do well at school was my contribution

Even though I had pulled the running away stunt during my Inter Cert mocks as the real exam loomed, my friend and I decided we would put in the work to get good results in the exam. Some evenings we used my house, and the kitchen table would be littered with past exam papers, A4 pads and pens. We figured that the only way out of a small town was to study and do well in the exam. I was in a serious relationship but the idea of marriage didn't become so important until after I left school. At this stage I still wanted to do well and we would spend hours studying, fuelled with sweets and drinks. At the weekends we would let off steam by getting drunk or stoned and going to the local disco or to hear a band in the rugby club or St Mary's Hall. We were too young to be served in pubs but we could buy a flagon of cider in one of the old pub/grocery shops in Connaught Street. Before we hit the disco we would go to the park and drink the illicit alcohol. We thought we were so cool, getting drunk or smoking grass, but we were tame by today's standards. For me, this was not only a way to have fun and to dampen the pain, but it also helped me feel normal, feel like everyone else who was going out. Even though I had missed some of my mocks when I ran away to England I still got good results, enough to let me know I could do well in the real exam. I was confident after most of them, except for the Irish, which I was weak at. My results were good, but as passing Irish was compulsory I didn't pass my Inter Cert. It didn't matter how well I had done in the other subjects, I had failed the exam. Totally disgusted, I used this, along with the need for extra money, as a reason to leave school. Working and earning a wage made me feel more grown up. I was independent. I wouldn't have to account for every minute of my day and I would have money. My thinking was not very rational – I had to clock in and clock out of my job every morning and every evening – but I did have money. My first job was in Broderick's bakery, where I spent the day wrapping bread. Not the most exciting job, but for me it was a taste of freedom from school, homework, study and the eyes of the nuns, who knew everything. I made new friends and felt free of the restraints of the school system. Eventually I got a job in Dunnes Stores, stacking shelves and helping at the check-outs. My boyfriend would sometimes meet me after work and we would walk home together, making plans for our future, altogether careless about the consequences of our relationship. I was living in La La Land. The parish priest's visit would change all of this.

My mother had been suspicious of my relationship for a while. She was convinced we were having sex, but I would never admit this to her. She could not abide this boy, although she would eventually grow very fond of him. Sometimes if she thought I was in the house on my own she would close the shop, walk up to our house, turn the front door key as quietly as she could and sneak up the stairs. She was hoping to catch me doing something I wasn't supposed to do, something that would give her a valid reason to bar him from the house for good. I wasn't supposed to have him in the house when she wasn't there but I had stopped doing what I was supposed to do. Being good did not get anyone anywhere. I had always been the good girl and look at how our lives had turned out. On one of these occasions she managed to get as far as the bottom of the stairs before we realised it. We were in bed together and held our breath, listening as she carefully crept up the stairs. When she opened the door the first thing she saw was me lying in bed, alone. Her intuition must have been on full alert but there was no sign of anyone else in the room or anything unusual going on.

'What are you doing in bed in the middle of the day?' she asked accusingly.

'I told you I was sick,' I replied.

She stood there holding the door handle, looking at me suspiciously.

'Why haven't you got a nightdress on?'

'I'm too hot. I think I have a temperature.'

I kept looking at her, afraid my expression would give me away or I would sneak a look at my boyfriend, who stood behind the door, his hands covering his nakedness. She looked around the room again. She never thought of checking behind the door and he remained as still as a statue, a mixture of terror and hilarity across his face.

'I don't know what I'm going to do with you,' she said. 'Get up out of that bed.'

'I'm too sick.'

When she left we fell around the place laughing at the relief of our near escape, not fully believing how we had gotten away with it. Now, as an adult woman with children of my own, I feel remorse for how I behaved towards my mother. Not so much because of my behaviour, but because now I know what it is like to be the person with sole responsibility for others, to be the one who has to carry on without any compass. But that day we laughed with relief and the complacency of youth. I didn't stop to think about how my behaviour impacted on others. I just wanted to have fun, to escape the feeling of being abandoned and unwanted.

Eventually my mother decided she would bring me to our family doctor to have a pregnancy test. I went willingly, confident that her suspicions would be proved wrong and that I would have the last word in the argument. As we walked to the doctor's surgery I remember thinking that this was a total waste of time. I couldn't be pregnant. It never crossed my mind that I could ever get pregnant. Don't get me wrong, I was not stupid. I knew that you could get pregnant by having sex, but there was a part of me that really believed this would not happen to me. I was too young. My periods had always been very erratic. They could last for two weeks or disappear altogether for a couple of months. As it wasn't unusual for me to have long gaps between my periods I believed this was the reason the doctor was admitting me to the local hospital. When we left his surgery that day I was even more convinced that pregnancy was not the problem. I can remember returning home feeling vindicated even though there was no pregnancy test result that day. I was admitted to the local hospital the next day. As it was only a five-minute walk from our house my mother popped in to see me most mornings when she was on her way to or from town or the Franciscan Friary church where she attended morning Mass. I can't remember how long I stayed there. It was boring, but it was also good to have all this attention. The days were spent eating, reading and lounging around. Blood and urine samples were taken and I chatted to the other women, who all seemed much older than me. One woman had had a baby and she asked if I would like to hold her. I did, feeling nervous in case I dropped the baby or didn't hold it properly. But there was no maternal longing in me as I held her. Babies were something for the future, for after I was married, not for now. When all the tests were completed I was discharged. I wasn't told anything about what the tests revealed and I was none the wiser leaving the hospital. I had not been sick. I wasn't recuperating from anything and I was confused as to why I had to be there in the first place. Maybe they would sort out why my periods were so erratic. But I wasn't told anything. I was a minor. Life continued as normal. I helped out at home, saw my boyfriend and waited for the day that I could leave home. Waited for the day that I could start my own family, one that was not tainted by all that had happened at home, one that we would get right.

'How are you, Jacinta?' the priest asked.

'I'm fine.'

'How did you get on in the hospital?'

So that's why he's here.

'Grand.'

'You know what I'm here for, don't you?'

'No.'

I'm not a mind reader.

'Greetings, you who are highly favoured! The Lord is with you. Do not be afraid, you have found favour with God. You will conceive and give birth to a son.'

Ah, no, that's not what he said. That was another representative to another woman a long time ago. What my rep said to me was, 'I came here to tell you that you are pregnant.' I can't remember if I was able to keep my poker face. I hope so. I was very young and I don't know if I had perfected my poker face at that stage. I thought he was here to lecture me about what my family thought of as an inappropriate relationship. It had never once dawned on me that I could be pregnant. To anyone reading this today that seems like a silly statement. How could someone not know that they were at risk of becoming pregnant if they had sex, especially if they weren't using protection of any kind? You have to understand that protection would have been hard to come by. This was the early 1970s and you couldn't get a condom in Ireland for love or money. Even later, when I was married, you still couldn't get a condom to prevent pregnancy in Ireland without going through the shameful ritual of facing the unhelpful chemist. All we had to go on regarding sex and sex education was street talk or what we were taught in school, and there the topic was either distilled into the language and images of biology or cloaked in religious dos and don'ts. Nobody ever told young men and women about the physical aspect of sexuality, the passion that surges through the body, or how the human body is designed to react to sexual stimulus. No one ever spoke about how touch can awaken sensations that are terrifyingly powerful and unfamiliar, sensations that were never spoken about, because bodily responses were sinful. No one ever taught us to recognise, respect and learn to control the powerful emotions that emerge during adolescence. No one ever taught us how to protect ourselves and each other emotionally, physically and psychologically. And no one ever talked about the fertility of young women, this also being a sinful topic. The education system was firmly monitored by the Church and sex education came down to the biological function of the body and the sinful nature of pleasure. No one could touch your body apart from your mother or the doctor, otherwise it's a sin and more than likely you are the sinner, particularly if you enjoy the touch. Is it any wonder that a lot of us didn't equate sex and pregnancy? Sex and pregnancy were the domain of the married couple. So, for me, even as someone who was flouting the teaching of the Church, there was some unspoken belief that I wouldn't get pregnant. It was as if I knew what the consequences could be but I didn't really comprehend it. So when the priest said those words it was a shock, and I really did hope that I kept my poker face intact because I hated the idea that he would know how I felt or what I was thinking. The priests in the parish knew enough about me and my family without knowing my inner thoughts as well. While I was preoccupied with thoughts of finding my boyfriend and telling him the news, the priest's words were beginning to penetrate. I could hear him saying, 'You know that this is the end of this relationship now. That boy will run for the hills when he hears this. You need to decide what you do now. You need to decide what is best for your family.'

His words were like noise in the background, rushing over the voice inside my own mind, which was telling me the opposite. All I wanted to do was find my boyfriend and tell him this news, never doubting for a minute that he would be happy to hear it.

'He won't run away,' I said.

'I wouldn't be too sure about that,' he replied. 'This is about your family now, and what you do for them. What you do for your mother'.

I didn't understand what that meant. What did he mean by, 'You need to decide what to do now'? Today that decision would include the option of abortion, but back then, even though the procedure was being carried out in England at the time, the thought would not have entered my mind, and as a priest he would never have suggested this anyway. But I was going to get married. I knew that my boyfriend wouldn't run for the hills. So what was he asking me to think about? I didn't realise it at the time but in 1970s Ireland women had little or no choice regarding their bodies, or the actions and decisions they could make regarding their bodies. He was wrong. They were all wrong. My boyfriend would not leave me because I was pregnant. When he was finished talking to me the priest called my mother down.

'Now what are you going to do?' she said.

As if I had any power over what I would do. It never dawned on me that day to wonder why she hadn't just told me herself. She could have told me when I came home from the hospital. We could have sat down over a cup of tea and talked about it. This was the measure of the power of the Church, and the environment that I grew up in, that she had to call one of the local priests to break the news to me. An angel of the lord declared … Maybe she hoped that I would be so upset at this news that I would throw myself on their mercy and ask for their help. Maybe this goes some way to understanding why I had such skewed beliefs about sex, sexuality, pregnancy, motherhood, the whole shebang. I don't blame my mother for that; these were the beliefs she inherited from her mother, beliefs she held strongly. But I wish we could have talked about it. I don't know how much my paternal grandmother had to do with the visit from the priest but I'm pretty sure that they were already working on the solution. My place in Bessborough House was probably booked before the news was even relayed to me. Even as the priest was encouraging me to decide what I was going to do, they had probably set the plan of my disappearance in action.

As soon as I could I left the house and went to find my boyfriend. Even though the priest's words echoed in the back of my mind I was sure that he would be happy to hear the news and that he would support me one hundred per cent. And this was proved when I told him. 'We can get married,' he said. 'As soon as you are old enough or your mother gives permission, we can get married.' I knew he wasn't going anywhere. I was fifteen. I didn't think past the fact that we were in love and that everything would be okay. The thought of marriage seemed like the next natural step, not the terrifying thought it would become after my baby was born. We went back to the house together and spoke to my mother. He told her that he would be supporting me and our child. We were in this together. He was there for keeps. I can't remember whether at that stage she said anything about me going away. As I have said before, memories are strange things and I have no clear recollection of when Cork or Bessborough House were first brought up. I'm not even sure I knew where I was going the morning we set out. At some stage the subject of places for girls who were pregnant, girls like me, was brought up. I also knew that being asked really meant being told. Even though I argued that there was no point, as I was going to get married and keep my baby, the shame that having me at home getting bigger and bigger every month outweighed any plans I had. I didn't feel upset about being pregnant but I was torn between feeling guilty about my mother's upset and feeling angry because no one would listen to me. Maybe the guilt was one of the reasons I gave in and agreed to go to Bessborough. I could have refused. Or could I? It's hard to figure that out now. Would they have dragged me there kicking and screaming? I'll never know. Instead, one morning I was packed into my grandmother's car, along with my small suitcase, which was in the boot of the car, and the long journey to Cork began. Not even my siblings knew where I was going. I didn't know either, and I didn't realise how life-changing this journey would be.

4

The Road to Bessborough

'The daughters of the land languish in
the permanent winter of memory.
A soundless cry that began the day
Demeter abandoned her daughter.'
    – Jacinta Daly, *Demeter Abandons Her Daughter*

My memories of the journey to Bessborough House are patchy, fragmented. It's strange, what sticks in your mind and what doesn't. I don't recall the details of the days leading up to the journey. I don't recall how that day began or who made the travel plans, I don't even remember packing my case. But I did have one and who else would have packed it? And I must have been included in some of the planning. Don't you think? 3 March 1973 was a bright crisp day, with clear blue skies and a cold wind. Typical March weather. I was fifteen years of age the day we pulled away from our house to begin the long drive that would bring us to Cork. I was about to undertake a journey and cross a threshold far greater than any physical or geographical one, but it would be years before I fully realised this. I had no choice in what was happening. I was doing this to appease my mother, to spare her the shame of everyone knowing her daughter was pregnant. But it seemed like a useless sacrifice, because as soon as my baby was born I was bringing him or her home and life would continue as normal. My coping mechanism, the one I had developed the night I was told my father was leaving home, the one that had kept me going ever since, was simple.

Ignore any uncomfortable feelings, act as if I took everything in my stride and never let 'them' know how I really felt. It had served me well so far. In later years when someone asked me how I got through my time in the home I would just shrug and say that I wasn't going to let those nuns beat me down. This was just another obstacle to be overcome, another hurdle to clear. I was like a steeplechaser, blindly jumping over these hurdles as they appeared without looking back to see if any damage was done, to me or anyone else. I didn't see what others closer to me may have seen; a young girl trying to make sense of a life that had become chaotic, trying to act older than she was. A young girl moving on without questioning what it was she was running from or running towards. Run as fast as you can, keep going forward, don't look back; these were some of my unspoken mantras. So I went along with the plan to go to Bessborough House. I didn't know anything about the place. I'd say very few people did back then, except for those who were forced to use the home. I would get through this, prove them all wrong (whoever they were), bring my baby home and get on with the rest of my life. I didn't take into account the effect that being banished from my family and community would have on me, or what the drip feed of toxic conditioning that imprinted the words 'girls like you', 'fallen woman', 'sinner', 'unworthy', 'unclean' and so on, would do to my psyche. I didn't think about the long-term impact of shame and how that would seep through every aspect of my life, affecting every decision I made from that time. What did I know about shame back then? I was so busy being the strong person that I couldn't see what was happening in front of my nose. I didn't even stop to think of what it would be like to have a child, to be responsible for another human being.

Though the memories of that journey are fragmented, I can recall what I felt on that March day. In one sense it seemed to be an uneventful trip, unlike the Sunday drives we took with my father or the trips to Galway each year, where there was something to look forward to at the end of the drive. I couldn't connect with my mother or grandmother's oohing and aahing over the scenery. To listen to the two women you'd think we were just out for a day trip, passing through unfamiliar country roads, towns and villages. In hindsight, it probably was a beautiful drive. But what difference did that make to me on that day when they were sending me away to the arse end of the country? None of us had ever been to Cork. When I was older

I would have more appreciation of the beauty of the Irish landscape, but on that day I was preoccupied with how I might get out of this situation. My grandmother drove and my mother sat beside her and they tried to include me in their conversation. I believe this was partly an attempt to keep the chat going, to fill the silence, and partly to alleviate the tension in the car. It was a long drive from Athlone to Cork, with no motorway, mobile phones, internet, video games or any of the other constant chatter that serves to distract and amuse these days. There was no escape from the confines of the car or the two women in the front seats. I sat alone in the back with plenty of time to think and imagine what it was I was heading towards. I wondered if my siblings knew where I had disappeared to. We had left very early in the morning. They would surely ask where I was when they came down for breakfast. My sister told me years later that she had asked where I was and my mother told her I had gone to England. The whole thing was ridiculous, as all my friends would soon know. My boyfriend would tell them where I was, which would put an end to the secrecy. But as far as my mother was concerned I would come to my senses and eventually come home alone from Cork and life would carry on as normal. It would seem that she too had a great propensity to jump over hurdles without thinking of the consequences.

There was a pair of pink wooden-soled Scholl's sandals packed safely in my case. I didn't need maternity clothes as I was as thin as a rake and wouldn't begin to show for months, but I had bought the Scholl's, even though they were considered expensive at the time, because they were supposed to help with varicose veins and everyone knew that when you were pregnant you could get varicose veins. It didn't matter that I didn't really know what varicose veins were, or how they affected people. I just thought that this was a good purchase and they looked cool. I don't know what it was about them but I felt good when I wore them. I liked the colour and the style and felt they were almost hippie-looking. They made a clip-clop sound when I walked in them, like the sound I made when I wore my mother's high heels as a child. My boyfriend and I went together to buy them. When I write this I feel an overwhelming sadness for the young girl in the back seat of the car that day, a small suitcase in the boot containing her pink Scholl's, no idea of where exactly she was headed and unaware of how her life was to change irrevocably. I think some part of me believed that my mother would change her mind, though it would be silly to go all that way and do so. But I didn't really believe that she would leave me alone so far from home. We stopped for refreshments. It was a long drive and my grandmother needed to have a break. At any other time this would have been a treat, but today it was only a short respite before reaching our final destination. The nearer we got to that destination the more my stomach began to churn, so I was probably grateful for any delay. If there was one thing I was not going to do, though, it was break down and plead or beg for them to take me back home, so I tried not to show how frightened I was. I would go to this bloody place and they would see that it was a waste of time. I was determined to bring my baby home when he or she was born. Any attempt they made to include me in the conversation was met with monosyllabic responses. Why would I pretend that this was okay? That this was normal? I was going to make them feel as uncomfortable as possible. Besides, all my energy was taken up with keeping myself together as the dreadful feeling in my stomach increased. I was barely two months pregnant at this stage. They could have waited a while before sending me off to the far end of the country. If they had even sent me to Dublin I might have had an opportunity to see my relations there. But that would never have happened. Dublin would not have been far enough away to hide the shame I had brought on my mother and family. I had to be hidden away as quickly and as far away as possible. All of my arguments had fallen on deaf ears. This was happening and there was no going back.

When we arrived at Bessborough House the first thing I noticed was the long driveway leading up to the main entrance. This was daunting enough, but not as daunting as the first sight of the actual building itself. What is it about institutions? They seem to exude an air of coldness and menace. There was nothing welcoming about this place, nothing homely. Mother and baby home my eye! The words mother and baby conjure up images of maternal bonding, unity and safety. Add home to those words and you have a place of love and security. But this place looked like a hybrid of convent and asylum, large and terrifying. I knew that once I stepped foot in the place and they drove away there would be no turning back. Even at that last minute, I waited to hear my mother say, 'No, I can't do it. You can come home.' But it didn't happen, and when I walked through the door, small case in hand, I was on my own. I don't even remember any goodbyes. As I crossed the threshold my mind was racing with thoughts of how I would get through the next few months. I'm not sure if survival was even a conscious thought, but it was to be the constant underlying reaction that kept me functioning during my first few weeks there. It ran beneath the first introductions, the first time I entered the crowded dining hall, the first experience of sleeping in a dormitory, the first doctor's examination, the first summons to the head nun's office, experiences I had to survive, to get through. The realisation that I was on my own was scary. There was no one to fall back on, no one to trust, no one I could go and cry to. Each day was a series of stratagems, finding my place and eventually becoming what I thought of as comfortable but what was, in fact, institutionalised. On my first evening I was still reeling from the shock of my mother and grandmother actually returning home without me. Some part of me still clung to the thought that they would change their minds and come back for me, but as the hours went on and that didn't happen I had to put on a brave face and pretend not to be upset or frightened. At fifteen years of age I was a mixture of defiance, rebellion and plain terror.

I was led down a corridor by a nun who was dressed to intimidate in her long black habit, full veil and wimple. When I was in secondary school the headmistress, who was a nun, dressed in a more relaxed manner, often wearing a skirt and cardigan or jacket and a less imposing veil. Was it only two years or less that I had been at school? Oh, I wished I was back there now. I would never complain again. The nuns here meant business and their dress code was only the beginning. They were here to supervise wayward girls, wayward girls like me. They put the fear of God in me, even as my rebellious, defiant streak rose to meet that fear. Every institution has its own smell and this place smelled familiar. It reminded me of the convent that was attached to the secondary school I had attended. It smelt of a mixture of flowers, polish, cooked food, and something else indefinable; the smell of quiet order, silence and silencing under the guise of reverence. The first indication of that quiet order came when the nun turned to me and said, 'Now, Margaret,' because this was to be my name from now on even though I would forget that constantly at the beginning of my stay here. 'I'm sure you're hungry after your long journey. You're just in time for tea. You can leave your bag here in this room.' She pointed towards a door that led into a parlour of some sort and I obediently left my bag behind the door. I wasn't asked what I thought of the name Margaret, I was just given it. She pointed towards another door. 'This way,' she said.

Just like every new arrival who came before and after me, when we entered the dining room a silence descended upon the room and the women who were grouped around the various tables turned to look at me with curiosity. The nun led me to a free seat at one of the tables and introduced me as Margaret. There were six chairs at each table, three on one side and three on the other. As soon as she left the women began to chat again, some throwing covert looks towards me as they ate their evening meal. I would soon discover that this was the last meal of the day and if I got hungry later in the evening I would be on my own. Each setting had a cup and saucer, a side plate, egg cup and bread and butter. Boiled eggs were the mainstay of the house in the evenings, or, as I would soon learn, lettuce picked from the garden, tomatoes, scallions, hard-boiled eggs, beetroot and bread and butter. An Irish salad. I really cannot remember what the food was like overall. It was basic and functional and supposedly nutritious food for pregnant women. It was only when I began working in the kitchen that I realised the distinction between the food the women were given and that which was sent up to the nuns' pantry. But for now I sat down, the new girl, the latest arrival, and tried to ignore the silence on my entry to the room and the looks that accompanied it. I thanked the nun for the boiled egg I was given and ate what was in front of me. God knows when I would eat again, or what I would get. At home, we always had supper before we went to bed. Cocoa with crackers and jam, or toast. I doubted that would happen here. I answered the hellos from the women at the table and some of the questions they asked. 'Don't worry,' one of the girls said to me. 'You will soon get the hang of things. It isn't that bad.' I swallowed down the fear and the tears and got on with it.

After tea I was shown to the dormitory where I would be sleeping. There were ten beds in the room. How was I going to do this? The only other person I had shared a room with was my sister. I wondered what she was doing now. Did she know where I was? I hadn't even known where I was being brought to, so it was unlikely she knew. I found out later that when our mother had told her I had gone to England she didn't believe her. How come no one had said anything about it before I left, she had wondered? She wouldn't leave it alone and pestered my mother until she flew at her in a rage. 'She's having a baby. She's gone to a home for mothers and babies,' she said, 'and don't ever mention this again.' My sister was dumbfounded. She couldn't believe what she had heard. She went to her room and recorded the conversation and my mother's reaction in her diary. When we were older we would realise that what we thought of as rage or anger was in fact deep upset, and my mother had been deeply upset that day. The next day, when my sister went to write in her diary again, the pages about the conversation had been torn out. Now it was my sister's turn to be upset, and it took her a long time to forgive my mother for reading and destroying the pages from her diary. In Bessborough, unaware of all this, I thought of her glee when she realised that I wouldn't be back. She would have access to all my stuff. No point worrying about it now, though, was there? First I had to figure out how I would get undressed for bed in a room full of strangers. Ironic, wasn't it, that here in a home for unmarried mothers, marked as a fallen woman, my biggest concern was how I would protect my modesty that first night in the house. When I saw the washing facilities I almost lost my life. A row of sinks filled one end of the room while a row of toilet stalls filled the other. How was someone supposed to wash themselves with all the other girls around them? How would I wash down there? How was someone supposed to go to the toilet knowing there were other people outside the door? It sounds ridiculous, but these were the things that worried me that first night. How we focus on the minutiae when trying to avoid the bigger problem. How would I sleep? How would I get undressed? How would I wash myself? As if these were the biggest problems I had to face. How would I survive? How would I push a baby out of me? These questions were left for the moment as I struggled to navigate my way through the first night at Bessborough. Tomorrow I would meet the head nun. I would be given a job in the house. I would begin to get to know the other women and girls here. For now my mind was taken up with figuring out a strategy for washing myself without exposing myself to everyone around me.

I didn't think I would sleep that first night but at some stage I must have drifted off. It felt so strange to be sharing a room with strangers. I was so used to having my family around, and it was frightening to be away from them, to have to fend for myself. Who would look after me? Who would I go to if I needed something, if I had a problem? When I woke up the next morning it took me a few minutes to realise where I was. An unfamiliar room, no poster of David Essex or Marc Bolan smiling down at me. Some of the women were already up, used to the routine of the place. I got out of bed, very conscious of the fact that I was in my nightdress in front of all these strangers. I found the toilet and used it, then made a big show of sorting out my wash bag while I tried to figure out my next move. No matter how liberal I thought I was, I was genuinely mortified at having to perform my morning wash in a communal setting. That first morning I managed it by doing a full top and tail while still wearing my nightdress. I don't know if anyone even noticed. Probably not. I'm sure they had other things on their minds besides watching the new girl wash herself, but for me this all added to the stress of being away from home. I would soon get used to this, and though the shy girl loomed large in those early days I would discover in the coming weeks that the only way to survive in an institution was to put on a front, pretend that I didn't care and hide behind a facade of bravado.

'Hurry up, Margaret,' one of the girls I had been speaking to the night before said. 'Morning Mass is at eight o'clock, and woe betide anyone who is late.'

Surely I didn't have to go to Mass? It wasn't a Sunday.

But morning Mass was compulsory at Bessborough. Our souls had to be redeemed in some manner. Back home my friend and I would go to the Genoa Café on Sunday mornings when we were supposed to be at Mass. We would spend the time eating chips, drinking iced drinks and listening to music on the jukebox. When we figured Mass was over we would leave and find someone we knew who had been there and ask them what the sermon had been about. Sometimes we even paid for this information, as it covered any questions we were asked when we arrived back home. In Bessborough there was no escape from Mass, and it was during that first morning service that I discovered how charitable the nuns there really were and how self-sufficient I would have to become in order to survive. Standing on the cold, stone-floored chapel as the elderly priest droned the service, I was suddenly taken by the strangest feeling. It was as if a band was tightening around my head, squeezing it until there was nothing else in the world, only this horrendous feeling. I didn't know what to do. I didn't know what was happening to me and I didn't know anyone well enough to ask for help. I tried to shake off the feeling but the band just got tighter. The next thing I knew I was being helped up from the floor, where I had landed with an almighty thump, just as I vomited. This was the beginning of my morning sickness routine, which lasted for several weeks and which always seemed to occur at Mass. The first time it happened I was scared. I had never experienced anything like this before. But it was explained to me that morning sickness was common in the early months of pregnancy, along with the advice that as I was responsible for getting sick and making the mess I would have to clean it thoroughly. Bessborough was all about paying for your sins, whether you were at fault or not. I don't know if it was just an extreme form of morning sickness or if it was the claustrophobic setting that brought it on but it made the first few weeks there very difficult. I had never fainted before. Back in school someone had spread the rumour that if you put blotting paper in the soles of your shoes you would faint and many of us had tried it at morning assembly. It seems such a ridiculous idea now. Why would we do that? To be sent home for the day? Surely it would have made more sense to pretend to be sick before coming to school and not wait to faint in the middle of assembly. I suppose the idea of fainting in the middle of assembly seemed much more dramatic and exciting than just performing for my mother, who ignored all such pretence with 'You're going to school anyway.' There were a few occasions when I had gotten away with pretending to be sick, even though she probably knew that I was just angling for a day off. Sitting in the kitchen with her I would watch as she prepared dinner or baked scones or apple tarts, the smells wafting through the room while we listened to Gay Byrne on the morning radio or to music from the likes of Glen Campbell and Luke Kelly, whom she loved. There was such a sense of comfort and safety in the warmth of these innocent mornings where the worst thing I had done was pretend to be sick in order to stay at home in the cocoon of the domestic setting that was my mother's domain. I wished I was back there now. When I came to on that first morning in Bessborough, the smell of vomit and disinfectant heavy in the air, and the expectation that I clean up my own mess and, worse still, remain there till the end of Mass, I thought I didn't know how well I had it at home and how well I had been looked after. I also realised that if I had known what an awful sensation fainting was I would never have tried the blotting paper ruse either.

After the Mass ended I was introduced to the nun who ran the kitchen. I had made it clear that there was no need for me to be here as I would be keeping my baby and marrying the father as soon as I was old enough. They probably didn't believe that I would be allowed to take my baby home and the pressure to have the child adopted was applied from day one. Like the prisoners who declare themselves innocent and demand to be released immediately, there would be no reprieve for me. The analogy with the prisoner is not too far off – women in the mother and baby home who were pregnant for the first time were referred to as 'offenders' in the past. Those who were pregnant for a second time were referred to as 'second offenders'. They were kept away from 'first offenders' in case of moral contamination. It was decided that as I was getting married and preparing for a life of domesticity the best place for me to work was the kitchen. Everyone in Bessborough had to work, although the home was paid by the State for each of the women who stayed there. And that didn't take into account the private donations. As my time there progressed I would discover just how much the nuns got out of this arrangement, compared to the women in the home.

'Do you know how to cook?' the nun asked me.

'Of course', I replied, cringing inwardly at the idea that she would think I was stupid if I said no, but realising that of course I couldn't, as we were not allowed to use the kitchen much at home. The kitchen was my mother's domain and no one was allowed to interfere there. While most of my friends could have probably completed some basic cooking or baking, we had not been taught, except for whatever we turned out in school, and I never had much interest in home economics.

'Okay,' she said, 'you can start by peeling potatoes and boiling them. You couldn't go too far wrong doing that, could you?'

I looked at the box of potatoes and the peeling knife with apprehension, too mortified to tell her that I had no idea how to do this most basic of tasks. Determined not to be bested, I began preparing the potatoes. I'm sure there was as much potato flesh as skin dumped in the bin that morning and I'm sure she knew I had never done this before, but I continued with the task. Before long I had mastered it and was delighted with myself. It's difficult to explain the variety of feelings and emotions that crossed my mind each and every day in Bessborough. How I could feel a sense of pride when I learned some new skill, while also being afraid, hurt, angry and resentful. How I eventually made friends with some of the younger girls in the home, while still wanting to go home. How I eventually became institutionalised.

But this is an honest account of that first day. Did I still want to go home? Yes. Did I secretly believe my mother would give in and bring me home? Yes. Did I feel good about learning to boil potatoes? Yes. By the end of the first day I was a little less terrified. I had held my own, in spite of fainting and being sick, in spite of having no one to look after me, in spite of being thrown in at the deep end in the kitchen, and asked to do something that I'd never done before but that a girl of my age should have been able to do. I mean, what's the big deal about boiling potatoes? Peel them, cut them up, put them in a pot of water, wait for them to boil, don't let them go to mush. But did I still hate my mother for putting me here? Yes. She could have taught me how to boil the bloody potatoes at home. Did I still feel I would not be staying? Yes. But when I went home I would know how to boil potatoes. As the days went on I would learn some more culinary skills. I was not expected to cook for the house, thank God, for their sake and mine. I was a kitchen assistant and there were days when I swore that if I saw another head of lettuce that had to be washed and dried, or a scallion that had to be topped and tailed, I would scream. But I did learn some basic skills, frying eggs being one of them. Don't have the oil too hot. And when they start sizzling away and the white begins to emerge from the transparent albumen, gently spoon the grease over the yolk, until it is covered over with a transparent film, and you have the perfect sunny-side-up egg. I began to feel a little less stupid in the kitchen. Like every institution, I began to find my place, to fit in. In a way that was scary, as it meant I was settling in, accepting the situation and becoming more used to the place. But to this day I always flip my eggs when frying them.

That first day would set the pattern for the days, weeks and months to come. The rigid routine of the day seemed to become more relaxed in the evenings. But the nuns knew where we were at all times. I found myself missing the silliest little things. Like being able to read in bed, something I did regularly at home, but something that was impossible when sharing a dormitory. I had always read. Books were part of the fabric of my life and, regardless of how wild I had become when my father left home, I never gave up reading novels. In my early years I had read the classic children's books – *Little Women*, *What Katy Did*, *Jo's Boys*. Then I had dipped into Enid

Blyton and, as I got older, the Greek myths, which fascinated me. There was something about reading, a way to enter another realm, to enter the life of another character, inhabit a different world and learn more about other cultures. I was lost without a book and, while reading was allowed in the home, reading at night would have to wait until I got my own room, something that would not happen until I had been there for a while. There was also the realisation that most of the other girls looked pregnant. They all had bumps and were wearing maternity clothes. I was just over two months pregnant and stick thin, and I didn't begin to show until I was almost at the six-month mark. I wore my own clothes. I could have been at home. I didn't fit the physical profile for this place. I had been taken out of my own life and found myself in an alien environment. Instead of losing myself in the life of a character in a book, I *was* the character and, what was worse, this world was the real one and I had to live in it. I wrote to my mother and asked her to bring me home. I was keeping my baby, so what was the point? If only she had not been so much under the influence of my grandmother. But maybe it wasn't my grandmother, maybe it was the shame she would have felt at having me home in my condition. Whatever the reason, she stuck to her guns.

On certain days a makeshift shop was opened in the house. It reminded me of the tuck shop back in school. It was run by one of the nuns and a girl from the house and stocked with the essentials like toiletries, washing powder and other items. When I had money, which was sent periodically by my mother, I would stock up on what I needed, and if I had anything left over I would buy sweets or crisps or a drink. It was like being back in school. The whole place reminded me of the school I had attended, which was also run by nuns. It's as if I had left school to live my own life but had been dragged back into the very same system. My world had grown so small. In the evenings we would congregate in little groups to chat and gossip about what was going on in the house. By this stage I had made friends with some of the younger girls. There was a room in the front of the house where we went to sew, knit, write letters and find something constructive to do when we had finished our respective jobs for the day. There were no classes, no preparation for childbirth, no efforts to build up the girls' self-esteem or confidence. We had to find ways to do that ourselves. One day, as a group of us were sitting around the long table in this room, another girl and I began to chase each other around the table. I don't remember what started this chase. It was something I hadn't done since I was a child. But the sun was shining through the window and there was such a sense of freedom in being able to run, to move around freely, to laugh hysterically for no reason. We were like two children, so caught up in the sheer exhilaration of running faster and faster, our big bumps moving along with us, that we didn't realise one of the nuns had entered the room. She had heard us screaming and had come to investigate. We probably did it to relieve the mind-numbing boredom of the place. That was one of the biggest problems for me there, from my fifteen-year-old vantage point. That and the lack of freedom, the inability to make a choice to go somewhere or do something on a given day, the knowledge that I couldn't make a move without permission. I often felt guilty when I read about the harrowing experiences of other women, particularly those who had been in institutions in earlier times. It wasn't so bad in Bessborough in 1973, was it? But when I look back now I can see just how damaging that lack of freedom, of choice, of any sense of having a voice, the deprivation of my given name really was, and how it primed women for a lifetime of shame and guilt and fear and trauma. The gates may not have been locked but there was nowhere for us to go. Society was the warden of our prison and the punishment was regulated by the nuns in the home and reinforced by the dictates of the Church. The nun stood there flapping her hand, a priceless expression on her face. You would think she had found us committing the gravest of crimes. She was so angry. Not in case anything would happen to us, but because we were carrying precious cargo and putting it at risk.

'Stop that now, girls! Stop that! What are ye like? Sit down. What about your babies?'

I look back now and I realise that she didn't really care about us, or our babies. What she cared about was keeping order. Like the Stanford Prison experiment, once you put the keys of the institution in someone's hands, that's it. The power to subdue and control these women, that's what mattered. But we were young, we were two of the youngest girls there. Not quite children, but not women either. And although back home the idea of playing chasing would not have occurred to us, the suffocation of the routine there made it an enjoyable way to pass the afternoon. It was also an act of rebellion, if only a small one.

5

The Story of 'Girls Like You'

'There is something about words.
In expert hands, manipulated deftly, they take you prisoner.'
— Diane Setterfield, *The Thirteenth Tale*

The imposing facade of Bessborough Mother and Baby Home soon lost its ability to intimidate me. It's amazing how quickly you can become used to a place, become so familiar with its walls, doors, passageways and surroundings. The house, which was opened as a mother and baby home in 1922, was run by the Congregation of the Sacred Hearts of Jesus and Mary. Since that time thousands of women had passed through its doors. The air must have reeked of the heartache, despair and loneliness of those thousands of women. In 1943 alone 75 per cent of the children born in the home died within the first year of their life. The congregation also ran the Sean Ross Home in Roscrea and a home in Castlepollard. Thousands more memories of pain and heartache. I was not aware of any of this in 1973 but I remember one girl who kicked against the regime of the home and was threatened with being sent to Castlepollard. 'You don't want that,' another girl from the house said. 'This place is like a holiday camp compared to there.' In my mind Castlepollard was forever fixed as a punitive, prison-like place even though I really knew nothing about it. As the home in Castlepollard had closed in 1971 the threat was an idle one anyway. The gates were never locked in Bessborough but that meant nothing. Even though we had a certain amount of freedom, we really couldn't go anywhere. The imposition of a rigid and monotonous routine and the restrictions placed on our bodies (they didn't belong to us any more, as we were constantly reminded, but were part of a wonderful plan to grow babies for other people), was as real as the bars of any prison. It's interesting that mother and baby homes in Ireland used the same elements of control over young unmarried pregnant women as were used on prisoners within the penal system. Every move was monitored, everything was known, and the nuns had a way of cultivating allies in order to glean information that would have outdone the Stasi in East Germany. An iron fist under a velvet glove, only the velvet glove image began to wear thin the longer I was there.

The occasional visits I had from my mother, grandmother and boyfriend were a welcome distraction from the monotony of the days in Bessborough and I really looked forward to them. Once my aunt and uncle came from Dublin to visit me but that was the only contact I had with other members of the family for those seven months, except for a surprise visit near the end of my pregnancy. When someone came to visit me it took up most of the day. The journey down and back was a long one, so we had to make the best of those days. My mother would arrive with my grandmother, which irritated me, but she had no other way of getting down to Cork. My boyfriend visited me as well but he usually had to hitch a lift. We hitched everywhere back then, so this was nothing strange, but Cork was a chancier option than Galway or Dublin when hitching a lift. When he visited he would have to bring a handwritten letter from my mother giving him permission to see me and take me into town for a few hours. We thought this was hilarious, as anyone could have written the letter, and it made him feel like a schoolboy, having to go before the headmistress in her office to present it. In hindsight, there may have been a phone call before the visit to make sure it was all up front, but we didn't think of that at the time. I can remember the giddy feeling of freedom and release the first time I went into Cork city with my boyfriend on one of those visits. We went to a café and I had proper chips and tea and buns. It was such a treat to get out of the house and so hard to have to go back. When my mother and grandmother arrived we also went out for the day, but these visits were different as I still harboured huge resentment towards both women. It was good to get away from the home, though. I'm sure my mother and grandmother were doing their best to be kind to me on those visits but all I wanted was to be taken home and that was the constant topic of conversation, with me pleading and them standing firm. It wasn't really fun for anyone involved. Once they brought my boyfriend with them. I couldn't believe it. I don't know how he managed to sit in the car for so long with them, but he was glad not to have to hitch that day. We all went out for the day but instead of enjoying the freedom all we did was pester my mother to let us get married. And I mean pester. I was like a child begging for a toy. I'm sure at the time that I meant everything I said, but when I look back now I'm grateful that she didn't give in to me. All I really wanted to do was go home, and the visits and trips into town made it harder to go back to the house. 'At least let me come back home with ye,' I asked. That wasn't ever going to happen. We went to a café, had our tea and cakes, and then I was brought back to my unlocked prison, to the boredom and routine of long, long days where there was nothing to do except claw your way to the top, become part of the system, become a seasoned, institutionalised inmate instead of the wide-eyed new girl. I knew in my heart and soul that I was not going to be allowed to go home, no matter how many visits were made. But it didn't matter, because I was keeping my baby and they'd have to let me come home at some stage. And in my fifteen-year-old mind, that was all that mattered. My boyfriend and I often tried to weigh up what the consequences would be if I just went back home with him on one of his visits. It's hard to explain what stopped me doing that. Perhaps it was the sense of having done something wrong that was constantly with me that stopped me going home without permission. I wanted to be *allowed* to go home.

Letters were another distraction, but as no one was sure of where I was I didn't receive any letters from my friends or the rest of my family. Sometimes my mother wrote. I suppose she thought it would be good for me to get a letter from home. I used to wonder if people thought I was terrible for not keeping in touch with them. Even when my friends found out where I was, I didn't have visits from them either, but Cork was a hard place to get to back then. They did send their well wishes whenever my boyfriend visited. One day, when I was working in the kitchen I was called out and told there was someone in the parlour who had come to visit me. I couldn't think of who it could be as I wasn't expecting anyone. I left the kitchen and went to tidy up, then hurried to the part of the house where my visitor waited. I couldn't believe my eyes when I opened the door and saw my father there.

Instinctively I ran to him and hugged him. I was sure he was there to take me away from this place, and the disappointment when I realised this was not the case took away from my joy at seeing him after such a long time. Maybe he did want to see me, but he was also there to reinforce the idea that it would be better to have the baby adopted and finish with the father for good. His visit, which should have given me such a lift, knocked me back for days, until I justified it by telling everyone how great it was that he had travelled over from England to see me and how that showed how much he loved me. Back then I had a great tendency to paint the picture in such a way that it suited my version of events, another coping mechanism that kept me going for a number of years. When he left I sobbed for hours. It felt like being abandoned by him all over again and the result was to harden my heart a little bit more, add another layer of insulation so that I couldn't be hurt or let down by others again in the future. After this I settled back into the dull routine of the home. I didn't expect any more unannounced visits. Banishment meant banishment, and my father's visit was the only surprising thing to happen in the seven months I was there.

Although I wasn't always aware of the nuanced undertones of the house I did see something when working in the kitchen one day that I couldn't deny. This job came with perks and sometimes I was allowed to cook a fry for myself on Sunday morning after Mass. Nothing extravagant, mind you. We had to keep eye on the budget. But I could fry a couple of rashers or an egg and sometimes I sneaked in a friend to share this treat with me. It was nothing like the Sunday morning fry-ups we had at home but it reminded me of those mornings. When I had been there for a few months I was asked one day to help sort out and put away the food order that had been delivered to the kitchen. This gave me a sense of importance and responsibility. Things like this were highlights in an otherwise monotonous routine. My sense of importance slowly turned to confusion and disgust when I realised that the order was divided up, with the best and freshest fruit and vegetables and meat going to the nun's pantry for their meals, and the slightly more worn, not quite stale, not quite out of date, but just on the cusp of it food going to the girls' pantry, for all those expectant mothers. But, not to worry, because we had our iron and our vitamin C every morning to supplement the vegetables that were not so fresh and the meat that was not so … in date. This was the first concrete indication of what the nuns in the house really thought of us. Though I was allowed the odd sneaky fry, in reality the girls in the house were not good enough to have the same quality of food that the nuns had. What made this worse was finding out later that they were paid for the girls' keep, whether it was through a local authority or private donations. That day in the kitchen was an eye-opener for me. Up to this I had resented the nuns for their silently enforced control and the constant pressure to give my baby up for adoption, but I had not seen any evidence of lack of care or blatant disregard towards us. I had put their attitudes towards us down to their Catholic beliefs, but now I began to see just what they thought of us.

It's strange, but I don't remember the names of any of the women I met while I was in Bessborough House. Then again, they would not have been their real names. I don't remember the names of any of the nuns I met either. It's as if once I left I decided to wipe the whole thing from my mind. But that is almost impossible to do and, while I don't remember the names, I do remember the faces of some of the girls. I'm also conscious that those I classed as older were probably younger than I realised. When you are fifteen someone in their twenties can seem a lot older, which is not the case. The majority of the women I met were not keeping their children. Some were treated as imbeciles by the nuns, deemed incapable of making decisions. Between the nuns, the girls' parents and their parish priests, the decisions were taken out of their hands. Others were shamed or threatened into leaving their babies behind. Some had decided to opt for adoption before they even reached the home, the prospect of trying to survive financially, emotionally and even physically too daunting to contemplate. Some had not even told their parents. It's hard to imagine now, but the moral and societal conditions of 1970s Ireland meant that the unmarried mother was looked down on. She had done something awful, something dirty, and she didn't deserve to remain in her community. No one pointed the finger at the system that drove her to a mother and baby home, but everyone pointed it at her. The term 'unmarried mother' says it all. You were not thought of as a single mother, but someone who had dared to become a mother without being married. Marriage was the yardstick against which we were measured, and everything in society was organised to make it more difficult for a woman who found herself pregnant without being married. I can't remember discussing my personal circumstances with the women

I met in the home. We all knew that everything was stacked against us and the constant message was that our children would escape that stigma if they were handed over to good families, even though we would always be marked as unworthy. We could give out about it all we liked but this is the way it was. In my naivety I thought I had a choice. I didn't realise it at the time, but if my boyfriend and his family had not agreed to support our child things would have been very different. A baby born outside of marriage just wasn't acceptable, and raising a child on your own was too difficult back then. Apart from the financial aspect it is not easy to have the whole of your community against you. While I was blindly holding on to the idea that I was keeping my child regardless of what anyone thought, I didn't reflect on the idea that for some adoption meant giving their child a life they couldn't give them in the society that prevailed at this time. I didn't think further than the fact that I was getting married and could keep my child. It never entered my mind that I would change as I grew older, that this whole experience would make me view my life in a different way, that I would soon realise the insanity of wanting to get married at fifteen years of age. I didn't think of any of this when I was in the home. I just put my head down, got on with it and held on to my resentment of both of my parents for abandoning me in this manner. I learned the basics of cooking and of becoming a little more self-sufficient than I had been allowed to be at home, so that I could begin a married life as soon as possible.

While I never saw a baby being forcibly removed from its mother's arms that doesn't mean it didn't happen. What I did see were mothers who were forced, through the constant reinforcement of the message of being not good enough, to leave their children behind. I remember one young woman who braved it out and left with her baby, only to have to return to the home as she couldn't afford to live in the city with her child. (The Unmarried Mother's Allowance wasn't introduced until July 1973 and it wouldn't have been possible to survive and look after a child without some family help or support.) When she returned to the home, broken, she had no other option than to admit defeat and hand her baby over to the nuns who were only too happy to take her child and put it up for adoption. Her sobs were heard throughout the house that morning. It was heart-breaking to witness this, and what happened to her was replicated in the lives of many of the women and girls who were in the home at the time. There was another girl who clearly had a learning disability, someone we referred to as having a handicap back in that time. She didn't know what was happening to her body, and her screams when she went into labour rang through the house. She was a terrified young girl who shouldn't have been in such a place. There were women who had been told by their own parents not to come home unless they came home alone; women whose parents attended Mass and prayed daily for their daughters' souls but who wouldn't acknowledge what was going on in their bodies, or acknowledge their own grandchildren. Then there was the girl who had been threatened with being sent to Castlepollard. We woke up one morning to find that she was gone. We never found out if she had been sent away or if she had run away. That incident was enough in itself to keep most of us in line. Violence is not the only means of forcing and bending someone to your will and the Church, State and society at the time had it down to a fine art when it came to unmarried mothers. I didn't understand then how damaging this enforced rigid routine was, that it was just as damaging as the more stringent and violent attitudes of the institutions of the past had been. I didn't realise how it paved the way for the message of unworthiness to be cultivated.

Beneath the facade of a calm, ordered routine lay a deliberate system of psychological brainwashing that was used to slowly drip-feed the idea that we were shameful, sinful and selfish, that we had somehow done something very wrong, and that our atonement could only be real if we were willing to leave our babies in the care of 'good families'. Sometimes what seemed like impromptu gatherings, but were really carefully orchestrated evenings, took place in the home. A few of us could be in a room together and one of the nuns would just happen to come along, and the evening then became a time for talking and sharing. The nun would proceed to introduce a topic for discussion or begin by saying she had something important she wanted to talk to us about, like love, forgiveness, repentance. She would go out of her way to put us at ease. 'Are you okay there, girls?' 'Do you need a cushion for your back?' she would ask, looking for all the world as if she was genuinely concerned for our welfare. She would settle her fat round rump into the best armchair, shuffling so that every bit of her body found purchase. And when she was quite comfortable she would look around at us, all the women, young and not so young, sitting waiting on her words. I often think now about how bored the older women must have been even to take part in this ritual. We all knew what was coming but because we had nothing better to do we stayed and listened. Regardless of the topic, there was always a sting in the tail of the story, which emerged from the questions asked. These questions inevitably turned to the women, the wonderful holy women of Ireland who, for some reason or another known only to God, could not have children. The ins and outs of this were usually glossed over. I mean, how could you explain it? All these good-living holy women who could not have children, when here we were, a room full of sinners, all bursting with babies. Did God make a mistake? Get us mixed up with one another? I mean, what kind of a God would do this? No, better to just leave that bit and continue with the story. Ignore it and focus on the tale of how these women, who went to Mass every Sunday, didn't fornicate, didn't break the laws of Church or State, and were good people, had something missing from their lives. And then there was us, girls like us, no different really from the other women, the good women, except that we had stepped outside the boundary of what was acceptable. We were not married. We had tasted the apple before we were allowed to. We did not fit in. It didn't matter what age we were, whether we were going out with boyfriends, whether we had had one-night stands, whether we had been raped or were the victims of incest. We did not fit in. In the story, girls like us were the fallen women. But, in a sense, we were also the heroines. Because if it weren't for us, these good holy women, who were part of legitimate couples, would not be able to have a baby, would not be able to have a family. So here we come to the rescue, into Bessborough House, where we are fed, sheltered, looked after, given a bed, hot running water. Charity cases. No mention of the State funding that paid for our keep or the high price we would pay for being part of this story. No mention of how, by giving up our babies, we were breaking up our own family unit. But then again, how could you be a family if you weren't married? As long as we were willing to leave a part of ourselves behind in order to answer the prayers of the 'good' family unit, we were wonderful. Sinners still, let there be no doubt about that, but wonderful. It's ironic that 'fallen women', 'offenders', could be the answer to someone else's prayers. But just in case we lost the run of ourselves and thought we were 'good' for doing this, we were reminded that we were still sinners. You are doing a wonderful thing, but don't forget, you're still sinners. This doesn't fully atone for what you did. This-Does-Not-Balance-The-Books. But it's a step in the right direction. Willingly leave your baby here and you will be doing something good, because girls like you have to go back out there into society with the mark, the stain of sin upon you. Now, for some of you, no one will know this, because you are here in secret. But inside you will know. You will bear that mark. But every time that begins to get you down, just remember that couple that you saved from childlessness. That was the story that was told repeatedly.

It's no wonder that so many girls and women were beaten down into giving up their children, children who would have been loved and cherished by their own mothers if given a chance. The girls who sat around the room while this morality tale was told were real living women with broken hearts and broken families, broken spirits. As the story of the 'girls like you' was told and retold it reinforced the idea that there was something wrong with each and every one of us. We were the defects in an otherwise good and wholesome society. There wasn't anything wrong with the parents who abandoned their daughters, or the Church who administered this story and upheld it, but there was definitely something wrong with us. Funnily enough, there was never any mention of the fathers, as if they were just a footnote to the tale. The ideas of good and evil were brought down to a war between 'good women' and 'bad women', and in this war, which was propagated by the Church and kept alive by State and society, women were pitted against women and men were not judged. When I realised this it gave me some understanding of why mothers in Ireland abandoned their daughters at this time. Who wants to be branded as the 'bad woman' by their Church and community? When I was older and I read stories about the Magdalen laundries and the horrific abuses that went on there, the beatings, the shaving of the hair, the bullying of the young women, I would say to myself, 'Bessborough House wasn't too bad.' Then I'd remember the stories we were sold and the psychological damage that was done to young girls and women who, whether they left their babies behind or brought them home, as I did, still carried that mark of guilt, still carried that mark of shame. If you kept your baby it was almost worse, because the guilt you felt for depriving these childless couples who, after all, were so good and hadn't sinned the way you did, could really mess with your head. Screwed if you did, screwed if you didn't. There was no way out, except to keep the head down and keep going. For a long time I did not think of myself as a survivor. A survivor was someone who had gone through some great cataclysmic experience, like the sinking of the *Titanic*, or the death camps of the Second World War. I elevated the term 'survivor' to the heights of life-and-death experiences. I didn't think of Bessborough House as a place to be survived, more as a place I was lucky to escape from. At fifteen, still in the throes of adolescence, still childlike in many ways, I couldn't believe I had ended up in a place like this and all I wanted was to be allowed to go home. I didn't recognise the trauma I was living through, so survival didn't enter into it for me for a long, long time. Not until I had to look in the mirror and face the impact of the psychological damage that was heaped upon us, leaving the taste of 'there's girls like you' in the mouth.

6

Mothers' Ward

'Don't open your mouth. You didn't cry when you got it.'
— Bessborough House, 1973

It's hot. Probably too hot to be out walking, especially carrying this big bump. I have managed to persuade two of my friends to come walking with me. They are nervous. They don't want to get into trouble with the nuns and they are afraid I might have my baby while we are away from the house. We're not that far away, though. We are walking the lane that encircles the house, a walk I have done several times before. But not when I was in labour. There is a section of the lane that hides the house totally and when we reach that part I can pretend that it doesn't exist. I can smell the wild flowers, the grass, that summer meadow scent that reminds me of childhood treks through the fields at home. The sun is warm on my face and the fat blackberries ready for picking remind me of childhood summer days when I would go out with my mother or my friends to pick the ripe black fruit. An old can or jar would be filled to the brim and brought home, then turned into jams or tarts. We would arrive home with stained faces and clothes and be given out to for getting into such a mess, but it was always worth it. I look at the ripened fruit and wish I was back there, innocently picking blackberries. Instead I am walking around this lane, circling the big house for the third time, trying to think of a way to persuade the girls to go around again. They are getting edgier. 'What if your baby comes out here?' one of them says. 'What would we do?' She's right. None of us is prepared for what happens when we go into labour. The only thing we have to go on is what we have read in books or seen on television. My pains aren't bad. I expected this to be much worse.

When I woke up this morning I knew there was something different. There was what I can only describe as a dragging sensation in the bottom of my tummy. Not quite a pain and not overly uncomfortable, but something was definitely happening. I had no idea what this meant. According to the doctor, who visits occasionally to examine us, I am near my due date, but nothing is ever explained so I don't know whether I should be worried or not. As the day goes on I decide to continue as normal and not say anything until I have to. I'm not going near Mothers' Ward until I absolutely have to. Even though it's Saturday morning, Mass is obligatory, but I feel like an old hand at this stage. I've been here almost seven months and I'm not as scared as when I first arrived. I can get away with missing Mass the odd time. All that would happen is a caustic giving out by one of the nuns and a lecture on atoning for my sins. Why had I been so frightened when I arrived here? I did not recognise this as the institutionalisation process that it was. First frighten you to death with their power, then allow you to have certain privileges, then encourage you to assist the new women arriving. All of a sudden you didn't know whose side you were on, who was right and who was wrong, who you were. The one thing I am sure of at this moment is that I have no desire to go over to Mothers' Ward. As the hours go by the dragging sensation begins to change into achy pains. My only knowledge of what being in labour involved was what I had seen on television and as I'm not yet screaming or rolling around the ground, I'm going to wait until this gets much worse before saying a word. I'm not even overly concerned. This isn't too bad. So far. When the film *Helga* was shown in the local cinema, a film they were given dispensation to show as it was labelled as a sex education film, the descriptions of labour and childbirth sounded much worse than what I was feeling. The local clergy were appalled that it was allowed to be screened and there had been a great furore, with ambulances on call outside the cinema for the fainthearted. Most of the girls who watched it swore they would never willingly put themselves through such a terrible ordeal. And here I am, on the verge of my very own Helga moment. But not yet. I decided to walk around a bit more before venturing over to Mothers' Ward.

Mothers' Ward. I had often wondered why it was called Mothers' Ward, as if it was a safe haven for mothers and their babies, when we all knew it was a place of separation. It was an ironic title for the building that took over the square in the centre of the home, the building in which you became a mother and then had your child taken from you. I'm not even sure whether that was the correct name for the building or whether it was something the women in the home had come up with. All I know is that I am not prepared for this. No one is prepared for this when they are fifteen. I don't want to go over there. But then again, did anyone? Well, that's probably not completely true, because going over to Mothers' Ward meant being a day nearer to going home, to leaving the house, to forgetting all about this place. It also meant being a day nearer to leaving your child behind. I won't be leaving my child behind when I go home, though the pressure to have my baby adopted has not relented. But going to Mothers' Ward scares me. You were only allowed over there when you went into labour. Apart from that we weren't allowed near it, and the fact that it is forbidden adds to the apprehension. Also, when someone went over there they didn't come back. While I didn't believe they disappeared, the fact that they never came back indicated that there was something different about that section of the house, something that changed things. We knew that when you went over there you had your baby, but no one ever came back to tell us what that meant exactly. There was no one to prepare us for what would happen. All we really had were tales and rumours. I knew I must not cry out when I was in labour, a point that was made several times during my stay here. 'You didn't scream when you got it, so don't scream when you're having your baby.' Labour was the penance for sinning, for becoming pregnant outside of the sanctity of marriage. Did that mean you could scream your head off if you were married? I knew I was keeping my baby so I shouldn't have been so worried about what they said to me, but that did not prevent my feeling apprehensive. What if they just took the child after it was born and I was too weak to stop them?

'I really think we should go back now, Margaret,' says my friend. 'What if something happens to you out here?'

At this stage we are at the section of the lane where the house is invisible to us.

'Okay. Let's go around just once more. Please. Then I will tell them I am in labour.'

I am desperate to keep away from the house. They agree to walk around with me once more, and I try to walk as slowly as possible, prolonging the last vestige of freedom. I don't think walking will do my baby any harm but we have never been instructed on what to do when we went into labour, except to let someone in charge know. All the lectures and instructions in the house were on our faulty morality, our contribution to 'good' childless couples and on how we were to pay for our sins. When we have completed the fourth lap of the house, I still don't want to leave the lane, but I know it isn't fair on my friends. They want to help me but are afraid too, afraid that I might have my baby right there and they won't know what to do, and afraid that they might get into trouble for helping me if anything went wrong. I am beginning to get a little anxious myself. What if all of a sudden I was overtaken with the most awful throes of pain and I couldn't make it back? My pains are still manageable, but they are getting stronger and I realise it might be safer to be nearer the house. When we get back to the main building I can see the relief on my friends' faces. I go to my room to get my belongings together while they go to find someone to tell that I have begun labour. I'm not really sure what I will need, my nightdress, pads, toiletries, something for my baby. There is no one to tell me how to prepare for this event. I am doing this on my own. When I am ready I go to find the nun on duty that day and she brings me across to the dreaded Mothers' Ward.

I am afraid, more afraid than I was on the initial journey to this place. I am scared of what will happen when I get there, scared that this might kill me, scared that I won't know what to do, and just plain scared of being so helpless. You'd think I was going to my execution, which sounds a bit melodramatic. I know in my head that I'm going over there to have my baby and once that happens I will be nearer to going home. But I have a feeling of foreboding, of walking into the unknown. And all the time, just as when I walked through the door of Bessborough House that first day, I have to maintain a facade of calmness, a facade of 'you are not going to get to me', a coat of armour that hides my fear, my dread, my mistrust of these people and this place. The girls are not allowed to come over with me and I feel very vulnerable and alone.

'Pop up there on the table and I'll give you a quick examination,' says the nun on duty. She is okay, well as okay as anyone here can be. I have met her on the few occasions the doctor visited and she didn't seem too bad. The table is hard and cold. She takes my blood pressure, listens to my heart and feels my tummy. She then proceeds to carry out an internal examination. I hate this. I hate the thought of her hand inside me, prodding, probing at me. And it is worse than usual as the pains are getting a little stronger now.

'No,' she says, shaking her head dismissively.

I am not at the stage of labour where anything is going to happen. She tells me that the best thing for me to do is run a bath and soak in it for a while. Have a bath! Can I have a bath while I am in labour? Surely I should stay here under the watchful eye of someone who knows what they are doing? What if I fall getting out? Or what if I have the baby in the bath? I don't know how this works. I don't know what is going to happen. But I'm afraid to disobey her. I need her if anything goes wrong.

'A nice warm bath will relax you, Margaret. But before you have the bath there is just something I need to do.'

She instructs me to lie over on my right side. I do as she says.

'Now, pull your legs up to your tummy and relax' she says.

I am expecting her to give me an injection, something to help with the pain. But instead of the sharp prick of a needle I can feel her pulling the cheeks of my bottom apart and then, to my horror, she pushes something right up my bum. Cleanliness is next to godliness and I am about to have my first experience of an enema. I have no idea what is happening though, and I'm petrified, unable to speak or respond. I've never experienced anything like this in my life. What is she doing? Nobody said anything about this in all the whispered conversations we had in the house. She doesn't explain what she is doing and as I feel the liquid coursing up my bum I am rigid. What is she putting inside me? How will it stay in? This feels like the worst torture. As I lie on my side enduring the humiliation, I know I am powerless. It doesn't matter how angry or frustrated I feel with what is happening, all I can do is lie here and put up with it. 'You didn't scream when you got it.' Never mind the labour to come, I can't even scream out against whatever it is this nun is doing to me. Nothing had prepared me for this. When she is finished and begins to pull the tube out I am terrified that everything will come pouring out of me. 'Just lie there for a few minutes, then make your way to the bathroom,' she says. How am I going to walk to the bathroom? 'Come on, now, you haven't all day to do this.' I feel dirty and frightened. I don't know what is inside me and I'm worried that when it comes out all the shit will come out with it. I don't realise that this is the whole point of the exercise. Cleanliness is next to godliness indeed.

I don't know how I will make it to the bathroom, which now seems ages away. How am I supposed to walk down that corridor, run a bath, climb into it, get myself out and dry myself, all the while holding this liquid in and trying to manage the ever-increasing strength of my pains, without collapsing, soiling myself or screaming, something I swore I would never do in this place. Am I supposed to even hold it in while I have the bath, or let it go and then have the bath? She had not been clear about what to do. They are all mad here. I hate them. I put on my dressing gown and slowly shuffle down the corridor, clenching my bottom. When I get to the bathroom I begin to run the bath, but I needn't have worried about the order I should do this in, as I have to sit on the toilet immediately. When I let go of the liquid there is no relief, only a sense of disgust, and it's painful, as I am having a contraction at the time. I wish my mother was here. I was going to pretend that I had the bath, but after the enema I want to feel clean again, so I get in as quickly as I can. I wouldn't have gotten away with pretending anyway as she is down the corridor after me to make sure that I am doing as she instructed. I get in and soak in the bath for as short a time as possible. I am so afraid. When I get out I wrap a towel around me, sit on the toilet again and eventually make my way back to the room. There is a sense of relief that this part of it is over with, but the pains are getting closer and stronger. Keeping my mouth shut in this place will take all my willpower and determination.

'Now you'll feel much better, Margaret,' she says.

I don't feel better at all, especially when I realise she is getting prepared to do another internal examination. This time she is happier with the progress I am making and all clean now, externally and internally, I am moved into the labour ward, which is just another variation of the room we have left with another table that is just as cold and hard as the one I was on earlier, but a little higher. There is a nurse there. Well, she's dressed in what looks like a nurse's outfit, but I have never seen her before and don't know who she is. Maybe she's a midwife? She doesn't speak except to answer any questions the nun puts to her. I might as well be invisible to her. 'Not too long now, Margaret,' the nun says, and I remember thinking that if my baby is born before midnight he or she will have their birthday on 2 September. I lie there, looking up at the ceiling and the huge light over the bed. I can see myself reflected in it, and I wonder how this happened. How did I end up here? And I curse everyone and everything that brought me to this place.

At some stage the nun has left for the day and I am left alone with the nurse. I'm not sure what time the shift change occurred but another woman has come into the labour ward. She is the night nurse, and she is taking over the night shift. At least when the nun was there I felt a little safer. She seemed to know what she was doing, but I don't know who these two women are. I don't think they are nuns and they look ancient to me, but then again, at fifteen people often look older than they are. I wonder if they are even real midwives. They dodder around the labour table muttering and throwing glances at each other. The day nurse had been preparing an injection for pain relief but the night nurse thought that I was young and strong and didn't need it. What happened next was almost as surreal as the enema experience, as these two women took up their positions each side of me and proceeded to have a stand-up argument over which of them was right. 'Jesus,' I think to myself, 'you couldn't make this stuff up.' The night nurse wins as it is her shift, and I am given two tablets and a glass of water for the pain. I don't care, I just want them to shut up and leave me in peace. All I want is for all of this to be over and to get out of here. They won't hear one word out of me. I won't please them. 'Fucking eejits,' I think, while at the same time asking God to help me keep my mouth shut if it gets really bad. I am trying not to let them see that my pains are getting stronger. I will not shout out in this room. It is not out of obedience that I am determined to obey the instruction not to open my mouth in the labour ward. It would be perfectly normal to shout out when you are in pain. Sometimes I wondered if the instruction was to goad the women, so that the nuns could accuse them of being weak. But I'm not going to give them the satisfaction of screaming or crying. I will show them how strong I was.

I don't like this woman, this night nurse. She is cold and uncaring and there is no empathy here. At this stage things are beginning to escalate and one of the girls who has already had her baby is drafted in to help me. Just as we are given jobs when we enter the home, as soon as you have your baby you are given a job in Mothers' Ward. For some this is working in the nursery, doing the day or night feeds, a cruel thing to impose on someone who has to give up her child. Sometimes these girls are called in to assist women in labour. Where today you might have your husband or partner, your mother, sister or a friend in the labour ward with you, at Bessborough you had someone who had already had their baby. Again, there was no element of choice in this. Just like the enforced enema or the enforced decision around pain management, the choice of who would be beside me during the birth of my baby was taken out of my hands. It could be someone you knew, someone you didn't know, even someone you didn't like. I don't know anything about this girl and she doesn't know anything about me, but we are stuck with each other for the remainder of my time in this ward. She is the one holding my hand and encouraging me to push as I go into the last stages of labour. I resent her for this while being grateful to her also. It's really happening now, and even though I am fully thrust into this experience a part of me is thinking that this isn't right. I'm not screaming and I'm not rolling around in torment. This isn't right. And it shouldn't be happening so far from home. I shouldn't be doing this on my own. But my baby is ready to come out into the world.

'Push, Margaret, push,' the night nurse shouts, looking down at me. 'My name is not Margaret,' I think to myself. I hate them all, I hate them all. I hate everyone who has anything to do with me being here. I hate these nuns, these women who work here. I hate my boyfriend. I hate my mother and all my family. I am alone in this. My daughter is born just before midnight, a 2 September baby. She is beautiful, but I only get a fleeting glimpse of her before she is whisked off to be cleaned and examined. Cleanliness is of huge importance here. I am so proud of myself, yet incredibly sad. I did this on my own. I didn't shout. But I wish there was someone here that I knew, I wish I had someone familiar to share this moment with. Instead, a girl I don't know is telling me how well I did. She is holding my hand one minute, then she is gone, following the midwife out the door to help clean my baby. I am not allowed to hold her against me, only allowed to see her for the briefest of moments. The babies are kept in a strict routine and being cuddled is not the main priority here. I lie back thinking, 'I've done it. I have a beautiful baby girl and I didn't shout.' What I had not thought of was that I might need stitches. Just two of them, but as the night nurse approaches me I can tell by her look that I will be punished for not shouting. I psych myself up for the pain, but it is too much. She hasn't numbed the area and I scream my head off, especially when she administers the second one, as I know what to expect. Thank God it was only two. There is no mistaking the satisfaction in her eyes. Nothing could have prepared me for the experience of being in labour in the Bessborough House. Nothing could have prepared me for the enema, the bath, the fighting midwives, the stitching, having to share such an intimate experience with a stranger. This is the punishment for your few moments of pleasure. This is an atonement for your sins. But I can afford to be smug in spite of my anger, in spite of my pain and loneliness. I've got through this and I have a beautiful healthy baby girl and I will be bringing her home with me next week when I leave this godforsaken place.

7

The Homecoming

'… to leave with a baby with no support was impossible.'
– MBHC Final Report, 2020

I didn't think I would sleep the night my daughter was born, but I must have nodded off at some stage. I couldn't believe that I had done it. I had my baby, without any family support, and I felt strangely proud yet profoundly alone as I lay there thinking about it. It had not been the horror show I anticipated. I had not let myself down in front of these women, whose only wish was to see me scream in pain, making full atonement for my sins. Well, I showed them. Until I had to be stitched, which I am sure was done deliberately in an effort to break me in some way. 'Who cares,' I thought, 'I'll be going home soon.' I couldn't wait to tell her father, to let my family know. There was a new arrival in our home and she was beautiful. She had looked so tiny, so beautiful. How could anyone think there was anything wrong with this? I didn't realise it, but there would be a lot of pressure put on me to change my mind, to have my baby adopted before I was allowed to leave the home. But that night, as I settled myself down, sore and tired, all I could think of was my impending journey home with my daughter. I had only been allowed to see her briefly. Then she was whisked away. Mothers and babies were not allowed the bonding process that is so important in the first few minutes, but we would make up for that. And even though visits to the nursery were discouraged, I knew I wouldn't be sticking to that.

When I woke up the next morning, I wasn't sure what to expect. I had a feeling it wouldn't be breakfast in bed. When I was in hospital in Athlone, which seemed like a lifetime ago, even though there was nothing wrong with me I had eaten all my meals in bed and could rest as much as I wanted. Things were different here. I had my breakfast in a room similar to that in the big house, with tables laid out with the usual cereal and toast. As I made my way back to my bed, still feeling weak and tired out, one of the nuns who worked in Mothers' Ward came into the room. 'Margaret,' she called, 'can you come out here and give me some help?' I automatically turned to follow her, still in the habit of obeying them. Unbelievable! What was even more unbelievable was what she asked me to do. We entered an adjacent room that had a row of empty beds and she asked me to help her move them to another room. I had had my daughter only a few hours ago. Now she was asking me to move beds! There was no let-up with these women. I knew that this wasn't right and I was nervous in case I did some damage to myself so soon after giving birth, but there is something about being brought up Catholic, being indoctrinated into the belief that nuns are somehow superior to us ordinary women, something deeply ingrained in us from the time we were children. So, in spite of the rebellious streak that had kept me going at times, and in spite of knowing that I was not a bad person, or a sinner, there was still that automatic inclination to obey her. And that is how I began my first morning after having my daughter. No breakfast in bed for me. Instead it was helping a nun move beds from one room to the next.

I couldn't wait to go to the nursery to see my baby. I wanted to feed her and hold her. But permission had to be given first. In Bessborough House it was a stranger who looked after our children, not the mothers. Someone else would be responsible for my daughter's care, for feeding her, changing her and putting her down to sleep. I don't know where I got the will from but I insisted on seeing her. If they wouldn't let me I was going to the reverend mother. One of the first things I had done was phone home. Bear in mind that this involved getting permission to make a call in the first place. Then you rang the local public phone box, hoping that someone you knew or someone who knew the person you were looking for would answer the phone. Then you would ask them to get a message to the person in question or give them a specific time that you would ring back and hope that they would be there. As mad as it sounds, it usually worked, as everyone knew everyone on the road and most people were good at passing on phone messages. I must have been really naive as it didn't dawn on me that my grandmother would have kept in touch with the home and my family probably knew pretty quickly that my daughter was born. Word eventually got through to my boyfriend that our daughter was safely here, that she was beautiful and that we were ready to make a plan to get home. I wished I could just go straight away, pack everything up, even leave everything behind. I didn't care, as long as we both got out of here. But arrangements had to be made. Someone would have to come down for us, and as far as I knew there was still the expectation that I would come home alone and spare my family the shame. I was not allowed full access to the nursery but I think they were getting the message that I wasn't going to back down, so as I was keeping my daughter it was decided that I could do some feeds. I was given instructions on how to make up the formula and how to change nappies. I was incredibly nervous but I wanted to learn how to look after her myself. At a certain time in the evening all access to the nursery was stopped except for those who worked there. Fortunately, the girl who had helped me through my labour worked in the nursery, and she let me know how my daughter was doing. I was lucky. Some of the women didn't get to spend any time with their children and, even if they did, they would be leaving them behind when they left.

One day when I happened to be over at the nursery I was told that there was a phone call for me. I thought it would be my boyfriend calling to finalise the arrangements for our trip home. There was no one else I was expecting to hear from. When I answered the phone the voice on the other end of the line was that of a stranger. 'Hello, Jacinta,' he said. He was using my real name so it must be someone who knew me, but I didn't recognise the voice. 'You don't know who I am. I'm a friend and I want to give you some advice,' were the next words. Who the hell was this? Some weirdo? 'Who is this?' I asked. I was confused, and getting angry. 'Please listen to me, Jacinta. I am a friend of your family and I am phoning to say that you are making a mistake in bringing your baby home. The best thing for everyone, including your child, would be to come home, have your baby adopted by a good family and start over. It would be better for all involved. You will never be able to give this child what they need. I'm telling you this in your best interests.' I couldn't believe what I was hearing. Who was this person? He refused to tell me his name and I didn't recognise the voice. Who did he think he was? My response was typically teenage. 'Fuck off and don't ring me again. Pervert!' I hung up but I was shaking all over. Who had that been? I couldn't ask anyone in the home. Maybe they had organised the call. Maybe it was someone my family had asked to phone me. He knew my name and that I had had a baby. What if they were trying to stop me keeping her? I would have to try to contact my boyfriend and let him know what had happened. I had to get out of here soon in case anything happened to her. I rang the local phone box and asked the person who answered if they could get a message to him asking him to ring me as soon as he could. I couldn't get home unless someone came down here to bring me home and that would not happen without the agreement of my mother. Permission to leave would only be granted if she gave the go-ahead. I couldn't even make the phone call to my boyfriend without coming up with some excuse to do so. Everything was examined and everything was known in the house. Looking back now it seems so ridiculous. I could have gotten on a train and gone home, couldn't I? But I was fifteen, I didn't have any money and I was out of my depth. I needed to do it right so there would be no misunderstanding or risk of losing my daughter.

The day my boyfriend contacted me and told me he had got a lift organised for us was such a relief. Now I had to convince my mother. I imagine it was the awareness that I was not going to back down that broke her down. My boyfriend had always said that if my family would not let me home with my daughter then his family would take us in. We were still together, still planning on getting married, so there was no reason not to bring our daughter home. As the day when we would be leaving came nearer I became more and more agitated. On several occasions I was called to the office of the head nun and she laid out all the reasons why what I was doing was a mistake. I was too young. The relationship wouldn't last. I would be back down asking for their help. Did I realise how difficult it would be to have to admit defeat and eventually let my daughter go? How would I manage financially? What would this do to my family? My mother? She tried everything in the book to get me to change my mind but I was adamant. We were bringing our daughter back home, where she belonged. We were not leaving her here. Just as I had every time I was called to her office, I cursed her under my breath while politely answering her arguments.

When the day finally arrived I could hardly contain myself. I'd like to say that it was excitement that fuelled that morning, but it was pure fear. I still didn't trust them to let us go. I had managed to meet one or two of the girls I had spent time with in the house prior to my daughter's birth. I wanted to say goodbye to them and wish them well. I think we always knew that we would not be keeping in touch. Our relationships were transient and most of us couldn't wait to get away, put Bessborough behind us and get on with our lives. I left anything I didn't need with these girls, anything that might be of use to them when they went over to have their children. I was only half-listening when the workers in the nursery gave me the final instructions about feeds, nappies, bathing. All I wanted to do was get out of there. When my boyfriend arrived I was so relieved. A member of his family had driven him down and the back seat was cleared so that I could sit there and hold my daughter safely. I can still remember him driving away from the house, down that long driveway towards the gate, while I sat in the back thinking, 'They're going to be waiting at the gate.' 'They're going to come after us.' 'They'll stop us further up the road and bring us back.' I can't describe the level of paranoia that drove those thoughts. The power these nuns exerted over us had me believing that I was getting away with something in bringing my daughter home. As if I had committed some crime and was now on the run. It was an awful feeling, and I'd say we were halfway from Cork to Athlone before I relaxed and finally realised we were free. Now we had to decide which home we were going to. My mother may not have stopped me leaving Bessborough but she had not given a definitive instruction to come home. There were no mobile phones, no way to check in as there is now. As we drove along the country roads, the same ones I had travelled with my mother and grandmother seven months earlier, we had to wait and see what kind of welcome we would get when we arrived in Athlone.

As we got nearer to home we discussed what we would do. We decided that we would stop at my house first and see what kind of reception we got. I was nervous. I had not seen my mother for a while at this stage. I had not seen any of my family since I had left for the home in March. I wasn't sure how much my siblings knew about their niece. Had they been told that I had had a baby? Had my mother decided to tell people once she knew

I was set on coming home? I was glad that we would have somewhere to go if we couldn't go to my home, but at the same time I really wanted to get back to my own bedroom, my own family. As we pulled up I was apprehensive. I got out of the car and went to the front door. My mother opened the door and I walked inside, carrying my daughter. I couldn't believe my eyes. All my family were there to greet me. But along with them were neighbours from our street and they all had gifts for my daughter. A woman who worked in a local factory had made baby blankets for my daughter, a next-door neighbour had bought a clothes horse, to help with drying the baby clothes. Instead of the cold judgemental reception I had expected, everyone was here to welcome both of us home. And from the time my mother met her granddaughter her heart was stolen. That is not to say that everything would be plain sailing from now on, but she definitely fell in love with her. It was such a relief to know that I had help and support, to know that I was not on my own. My aunt from Galway arrived by train one day to see her grand-niece. She had knit a beautiful dress for her, a labour of love, as she put it.

There were so many women and girls who never got the opportunity that I did, who didn't get to see their children again for many years and some who never saw their child again. Coming home with my daughter would bring its own problems as we all tried to find our place in this new situation, but the most important thing was that she would know who all her family were. She would grow up knowing her roots, her heritage, her kin, on both sides of her family. We settled into a routine of sorts. She was just as indulged and spoilt by her father's family as she was by mine and they all agreed that it would never have been right to leave her behind. The first few weeks were a steep learning curve for myself and my mother. When it was time to change her formula we had to call on a neighbour who had young children for help. I didn't know what to do and my mother couldn't remember. But with the help of this woman we managed to manoeuvre our way around any challenges we were unsure of. It was only when I was at home that I discovered who the mysterious phone call had come from the week before I left Bessborough House. My grandmother had a friend, a local doctor who had some involvement with the adoption board. It was he who had phoned me, probably at her suggestion, in a last-ditch attempt to get me to change my mind. A classic example of Church and State working hand-in-hand in an attempt to hide the pregnancies of women in Ireland and hide away the children born outside of marriage. But we were home. My daughter didn't have to be hidden away. Everything was good in the world, but it wasn't long before I met that judgemental attitude I had expected. Not everyone agreed with my decision to keep my daughter. One evening, while wheeling her buggy around the local park, I was followed by a group of young children. They brazenly asked me if I was taking my bastard out for a walk. I knew they had not come up with this term on their own, that it was something they had heard at home, and I thought I was very smart when I told them a 'bastard' was someone who had no father and as she had a father and everyone had a father somewhere, it was impossible that there was such a thing as a bastard. I don't know who was worse, me or them. On another occasion my sister overheard a neighbour refer to me as a Jezebel when she spotted me out walking with my daughter. She quickly gave out to her for calling me names and the woman walked away, tut-tutting under her breath. It was 1973. There were always going to be some people who were going to judge.

The last mother and baby home didn't close until the late 1990s and there was still an air of judgement in relation to unmarried mothers. Even though I had been welcomed home that didn't mean I was fully forgiven. I could deal with that but I was beginning to realise that I now had another problem to deal with. I didn't feel the same way about my daughter's father as I had before I went to Bessborough. I didn't want to get married, and I didn't have the language to verbalise how I felt or to even explain it to myself. I just knew that, engagement ring or not, something inside me was pushing against the idea of marriage and lifelong commitment. And no wonder. I had my sixteenth birthday just over a month after I came home from Bessborough and I had been through a life-changing experience. I didn't say anything to my boyfriend at first. I thought maybe it was something to do with having the baby and that things would get back to how they had been if I gave it a bit of time. He was besotted with his daughter and his family were very supportive. My family also seemed to have backed off on the idea that I should finish with him. I didn't know what to do. It wasn't like today where a woman can decide to raise her child herself and there is not as much pressure to stay in a relationship. Besides, I was not a woman, I was a child. What brought things to a head was the day when I realised I had an even bigger problem, far bigger than deciding whether I was still in love or not. I had always said that there would be no more sex until I was married, but as I hadn't said anything about my reservations regarding marriage my boyfriend thought there was no problem with having sex. He missed me. We were going to get married. He would be careful. Giving in to this is the biggest mistake I made at this time. Actually, not speaking out about how I really felt is probably the biggest mistake I made back then. But no one had taught me to speak out. No one had taught me to verbalise how I felt, or even to understand how I felt. So I went along with things, almost pretending to myself that we were getting married, when deep inside, I was full of doubt. Then one day as I was passing the local oil depot on my way up town I had a wave of nausea and felt as if I was going to faint, just like the feeling I had during the morning mass in Bessborough, and I knew. Even though I tried to convince myself that it couldn't be happening, I knew. And in that moment I knew that I couldn't do this again. Couldn't face my mother. Couldn't face another stint in a mother and baby home. Couldn't get married and settle down with two children at sixteen years of age. I didn't know what I was going to do but I couldn't face any of these options. I had managed to get work in a local shop since I had come home and everything was beginning to work out for me. Now I was right back in the same situation again and I couldn't believe it. How could I have been so stupid? In Bessborough girls who were pregnant for the first time were 'fallen women' or 'first-time offenders'. Being pregnant for a second time was almost like having a criminal record. How was I going to handle this? There was no one I could turn to. My first reaction was to tell my boyfriend. He didn't seem to mind that much but I was the one who would be at home with two children, married at seventeen when I should just be starting my life. I felt like a rat trapped in a maze. I backtracked afterwards and told him I had made a mistake. I was not pregnant. Shortly afterwards I set about making a plan that would change everything and affect all of us for years to come.

8

Finding the Words

'… when I'm able to talk I imagine that I won't be so alone.'
                                    – Edna O'Brien, *The Lonely Girl*

August 2017

The sun was shining as I walked into town. I wondered how I had gotten to this day, this time, this situation. I felt fragmented, split in two, a woman of almost sixty years of age walking resolutely towards my destination, my sixteen-year-old self hovering somewhere above me, encouraging me to go on. Their ongoing debate, which had become a familiar backdrop to my life over the last few days, accompanied me, though all any passer-by would see was a lone woman, making her way resolutely to her destination.

'Should I go ahead with this plan?'

'You're mad if you think this will end well.'

'Should I tell him at all?'

'Should I pretend there was another reason for arranging this meeting?'

These were some of the thoughts moving back and forth in my head. I was the one who had organised this day and the consequences would be on me. 'Go ahead,' the sixteen- year-old voice whispered. 'You've waited too long. If you don't do this today you will never do it.' In spite of the conflicting thoughts and the fear and anxiety this day would produce there was a part of me that believed absolutely that this was the right thing to do. I also knew that even though I was dreading this meeting, if he didn't turn up to meet me I would find him and tell him what I needed to tell him. I had carried this secret for far too long. It was time to let it go. The repercussions could be devastating. I thought again of all the reasons I had for not saying anything. There was a chance that I would lose the relationship I had with my eldest daughter, and possibly with my grandchildren. What would they think of me when they realised what I had kept hidden from them? Would they hate me? Would they look at me differently? The shame of being pregnant, of being sent away to Bessborough, still haunted me, and the double shame of discovering I was pregnant a second time was too much even to think about. What if the people I knew looked at me differently when they found out? What would my friends think? Because, once I told him, the chances were that everyone would know eventually. Times had changed and today single women could have children without worrying if they were married or not or whether they were even in a relationship. But knowing how things had changed didn't change the fact that I still carried within me that subtle element of shame that unmarried mothers in the 1970s had been forced to bear. I also knew that if I didn't say something soon, I was liable to erupt. It had been seeping up from some deep hidden place for a number of years now and my fear was that one day it would just explode, come rushing out, with devastating consequences. No, better to do this the right way, tell him, then my daughter, then the rest of the family. So there were really two of us walking towards this meeting that would finally put the past to rest. My present self who had carried her secret for over 40 years and my younger self, the ghost of the young girl who had gone through so much in the 1970s, who was finally finding her voice. Just as the journey to Bessborough House all those years ago had brought such huge changes to my life, I knew this shorter journey today would change everything for those around me also.

9

Second Offences

'… there was much less certainty that mothers who had given birth
to a second or subsequent child were capable of rehabilitation.'
— MBHC Final Report, 2020

When I realised I was pregnant again I was devastated. I was terrified and
I didn't know what I was going to do. How had this happened to me? And
I don't mean the physical manner of getting pregnant, but how could I have
been so stupid? Why had I listened to my boyfriend? Why had I not gone
with my gut? Not that he thought he had done anything awful. As far as he
was concerned, we were heading for the altar and having another baby would
not make any difference to that. Back then getting married so young was
acceptable, as was the age gap. My resistance to getting married, which had
begun even before I realised about the second pregnancy, was heightened a
million times now. What was wrong with me? Nobody could be that stupid,
could they? Most of my friends were sexually active, but none of them had
ended up pregnant. That was my foremost thought. Stupid, stupid, stupid
girl! The seeds of guilt and shame, the sense of responsibility, the habit of
taking the blame, which were part and parcel of being brought up Catholic,
had been fully fed and watered by my experience in Bessborough. It didn't
dawn on me to blame anyone but myself. I also realised that I was going
to be even more alone in dealing with this than I had been the first time.
I couldn't tell my mother. How could I ask her to take on another child?
She loved her granddaughter but still believed that being pregnant outside

of marriage was a sin. I don't know how she managed to find a way to accept this the first time; possibly because she loved her granddaughter so much and had done from the minute she laid eyes on her, but there was no way I could hint to her that it had happened again. She also saw the impending marriage as some sort of redemption for the situation. That had been one of the factors that made it easier for me to stand my ground and refuse to give my daughter up for adoption, that and the support of my boyfriend and his family. I couldn't turn to my mother this time, there would be no help from that quarter, and I didn't particularly feel that I deserved any. I wasn't sure whether to say anything to my boyfriend at first. I guessed that he would not be fazed either way, and when I did tell him that I was late and I thought I might be pregnant his reaction was exactly what I expected. We were getting married and it would be okay. There was no need to worry. All his swimmers were fine. But I was just sixteen and this was not the life I had envisaged for myself.

My daughter was only four months old and I had hardly got used to the fact that I was a mother. All my friends were still in school. Not that I saw much of them. I felt awkward around them. My life was so different. They were dating, going out at the weekends, living the free and single lives that sixteen-year-olds are supposed to be living, seemingly without any major responsibilities. I didn't know who I was any more and now I had to try and figure out what to do, what was the best action for everyone involved. It was all happening too fast, as if someone had taken over my life and turned it into a runaway train. What choices did I have in any of this? I went over it again and again in my head. If I told my mother she would be devastated. There was no way she would let me bring a second baby into the house, especially if I told her I wasn't sure about marriage. She would probably want me to go back to Bessborough and this time come home alone. Going back there was out of the question. If I had felt judged the first time I was there it was nothing to the judgement that was meted out to girls or women who had been pregnant a second time. Rapists – and rape was exactly what had happened to some of these girls – were not judged as severely. I could go ahead and get married as we had planned but I didn't want to. I can't even explain it, but every time I thought of it I felt like a trap was closing over my head. I believed love was the main reason for getting married and I didn't feel that for my boyfriend now, not as I had at the beginning. I could run away. But where to? Where could I go at sixteen with a daughter, a failed Inter Cert and no prospects? My head was exploding. I was trying to carry on as normal, as if nothing was wrong, but inside I felt that this was my own fault, that I had done something terrible. I was thinking like a 'second offender', like someone who had got caught committing a terrible crime. The one thing I was sure about was that I didn't want to get married. In spite of all the uncertainty I was facing I knew in my heart that this would be unfair to me, my boyfriend and my children. I didn't believe it would ever work. That left me with the only option, throw myself on my mother's mercy, probably end up back in Bessborough and have my baby adopted. But I didn't want to do this either. 'Oh God,' I thought. 'What am I going to do?' I didn't want anyone to know what was happening. It was too shameful, too wrong, which meant I was shameful and there was something very wrong with me. Bessborough had really done a number on me. If I had not felt worthless before I had gone through its doors, I definitely did now. But this situation was not going to go away, and sooner or later I would have to make a decision.

When I had come home from Bessborough I had started to work in a local shop near my home. The couple who ran it had known my father and were very kind to me. I went to work each day, looked after my daughter, spent time with my family, my friends, my boyfriend, all the time keeping the knowledge of my pregnancy to myself. My boyfriend had started working on the railway and when I met him some evenings the smell of diesel from him almost did me in. For some reason the smell of any oil turned my stomach. That is how I had first realised that I was pregnant. I often thought of just telling him there and then, but then the idea that I would be forced into marriage would stop me. I think at that stage my mother would have been happy to see me married and off her hands, and I wouldn't have blamed her either. I had no idea what I was going to do. Then one day I remembered that there was someone living in Athlone who knew my father and the woman he had left with. Maybe they would help me make contact with him? Even having an idea of some way out brought a little relief. But it would mean I would have to tell this person that I was pregnant. It was a risk and I was not sure how it would work out, but if I could make contact with my father and he knew all the circumstances, surely he would help me? Surely he owed me that much? I also knew I would have to bite the bullet and break up with my boyfriend. I had been putting this off. I believed he loved me and he loved our daughter but I didn't feel the same. If I married him I would have some sort of security but it couldn't be right to stay with someone just for that reason. And I couldn't pretend. I had told him that I had made a mistake and my period had arrived and I was afraid that if he knew I was pregnant he would wear me down and I would give in and take the easy way out. How does it happen? One day you are madly in love with someone, totally obsessed with them and feel your life would not be worth living without them and then, suddenly, all those feelings change. Maybe it was after being in Bessborough House. I had thought at first that it was something to do with having a baby, but having a baby and having a baby in a mother and baby home are two very different experiences. The level of shame and guilt, the experience of abandonment and psychological abuse changes you. Or maybe it was just part of normal teenage life, something that happens naturally, falling in and out of love with different people without really knowing what love is. Not that there was anyone else I was interested in. I had enough problems and had had it with men at this stage.

I really don't remember all the details of the break-up. One of my siblings told me years later that I was very cold to him when he called to the house to see if he could change my mind. She didn't know what I was grappling with at the time. I had a far bigger problem on my mind. In 1970s Ireland being pregnant outside of marriage was a huge problem and it was the girl who was tarnished with the label of 'slut', 'sinner', 'degenerate'. To have this happen a second time was to be labelled a hopeless and morally weak person. While I may not have spent time consciously thinking of those labels, my feelings of shame were probably exacerbated by those attitudes. I could not have explained it, but I wanted to crawl into a hole and hide from the whole thing. Once I told him I didn't want to continue with the relationship I didn't want to think about it or talk about it again. I was afraid that if he pushed me I would change my mind. The next step was to contact this person who knew my father and try to get word to him that I needed his help. One night I called to this person's house. She was surprised to see me when she opened the door. 'Hi,' I said, 'there's something I need to ask you.'

'What is it?' she asked.

'I need to get my father's address. I need to contact him and I was wondering if you would have it.' She looked at me with scepticism. She probably remembered all the evenings my siblings and I had harassed the woman my father lived with now, throwing mud at her washing and trying to rip my father's car tyres open when he parked outside her house. She probably knew that I had turned up at my father's door when I had run away with my boyfriend. I asked her to hear me out. I didn't want to cause any trouble. I really needed to contact him, and it was urgent. I needed his help with something. She asked me what it was and as I looked at her I thought to myself, 'Here goes, I am going to have to trust someone with this secret if I want to get some help.' So I told her. Told someone who was really a stranger to me that I was pregnant and that I couldn't bear to go back to that awful place in Cork, that I couldn't bear to get married either, and the only option I could see was to get away to England, away from my immediate family, until I could figure out what to do. To my surprise her expression softened and she said that she would see what she could do. She couldn't promise me anything and she was not going to give out his address without asking him first, but she would make contact with him and tell him what I needed from him.

'If he is willing to help me, would you ask him to write to me, but not mention the pregnancy?' I asked. If he wrote and asked me to come over to him to work for him that would give me a good reason to leave for a few months. She agreed to do this and when I left her house I felt a little better. There was nothing else I could do for now. I would just have to wait, carry on as normal, hiding my pregnancy, pretending my life was fine until I got a response. And if I didn't get one I would have to come up with another plan, possibly face everyone with the truth, and that seemed to be the most unbearable outcome.

A week later I received a letter. My mother wondered who it could be from, who would be writing to me. It was obvious that it was a personal letter by its white envelope and handwritten address. It was from my father and he was asking if I would be interested in coming over to work for him in the pub for a few months. He needed to fill a temporary position and he felt I had gained experience from my time helping him in the shop and from my present work. I wouldn't have to pay for room or board. I felt a mixture of relief and guilt as I read it. My mother couldn't understand why he would be doing this. We never heard from him and now he was asking me to come over and work for him. It was very strange and I think she presumed I would say no. Here was the letter I had asked for, but in order to follow through I would have to lie. I would have to act surprised, pretending to take the time to weigh up the pros and cons and discuss it with my mother. All the time I was thinking that I would be going over to him as soon as I could. Time was of the essence now. I was worried that someone would realise I was pregnant. While I wasn't showing yet, I knew it was only a matter of time before it would become more obvious. The only thing on my side was that I was thinner than I realised so I didn't show for a number of months. I was counting down the days until I could leave. I wrote back and accepted his offer. I used the extra money I would make as an incentive for my mother to agree to the venture. Did she guess? Did she know, on some subconscious level? I was asking her to take over full care of my daughter while I was away. It's hard to believe she didn't guess, but if she did she didn't say. It was agreed that I would go and I wrote back and thanked him for the offer. The fact that I was going to my father must have been very hurtful to her, but I couldn't bring myself to tell her the truth. I felt so ashamed of myself. Maybe I was taking the easy way out but it didn't seem so at the time. I had to go to great lengths to organise this, never mind the deceit involved. We all lie to our parents on occasion but this was on a whole new level. I would have to give in my notice at the shop where I worked. Before I had a chance to do this the owners approached me with a proposition they wanted me to think about. They were wondering how I would feel about returning to education. They were not offering charity, but an opportunity to go back and complete my Leaving Certificate while continuing to work for them. They felt I had missed out when my father had left. I couldn't believe that I would have to turn this opportunity down. I thanked them profusely and asked if I could think about it and get back to them. They were offering me a way out, a chance at education, but I knew I couldn't take it. Was there any way I could have come clean then, gone back to school and kept my baby? I don't think so. Eventually I had to tell them that I had decided to go to England and work with my father instead. I'm not really sure what they thought of that, but I felt I had no choice at this stage. The irony of it. Alanis Morissette missed out on that one.

By the time I was ready to get my flight to England it was becoming a struggle to hold myself in. I was conscious of putting on weight but I wanted to time the trip to England so that I would be spending the shortest amount of time away from my daughter. I had not thought of anything beyond getting there. I had not considered what I would do about my pregnancy. Adoption was not something I gave much thought to, even though I couldn't see myself arriving back home with a baby either. The night before my flight I was upstairs packing my case when I heard a knock at the front door. I couldn't believe it when I heard my grandmother's voice downstairs. 'Is Jacinta here?' I heard her say. What was it about this woman? She must have some sort of sixth sense. I went down to say hello to her. 'Your aunt sent over some clothes and there was a dress that I thought would be perfect for you.' My aunt from America often sent clothes over so there didn't seem to be anything unusual about my grandmother's visit. I thanked her, saying that I would pack it and bring it with me. 'Try it on,' she said, 'I'd like to see it on you.' She was eyeballing me as she said this.

'She couldn't know,' I thought.

I didn't want to try the dress on and have to parade in front of them in it, but then my mother chimed in, saying, 'Go on, it looks lovely.' I brought the dress upstairs to my bedroom. I would try it on, tell them it was lovely and pack it away in my case. But just as I was closing the buttons I heard footsteps on the stairs. My grandmother walked into my room scrutinising me as I continued closing the dress. It fit okay, and apart from putting some weight on I didn't think I looked pregnant. 'Let me look at it,' she said. As I stood before her she said, 'You're pregnant again, aren't you? I can tell by looking at you.'

'No, I'm not,' I responded. But she was insistent and I knew she could tell by looking at me. In the end I had to admit it.

'Does your mother know?' she asked.

'No', I replied,' 'and please don't say anything. Daddy knows and he is going to help me.'

'Go down and tell her. She needs to know this.' I knew there was no point in pleading with her. I had to go down and tell my mother the real reason for my going away. I had been so close. Just one more night. I explained to my mother that I hadn't wanted to burden her with this. I could see the disappointment on her face, the shame and the bewilderment. How had she ended up with a daughter like me? My grandmother more or less said what was done was done and it was better for me to go away like I had planned. How the hell had she known? It was only afterwards that I realised my father had told her, and not just her, but most of his family. When I found this out I should have been angry and I probably was somewhere deep within me. But I was so worn down. It was like the time I was in Bessborough with the nun when she gave me the enema, without a word of explanation. It didn't matter how angry or upset I was, I needed her. It was the same with my father. He had betrayed my confidence but I needed him. You couldn't trust any of them. There had been a part of me that believed he would keep my secret, but he hadn't, and there was nothing I could do about it. I didn't know any of this the night my grandmother arrived with what was probably the first dress she could find that would fit me, using it as an excuse to see for herself. So now I was heading off to England with the knowledge that my shameful secret was out there, known by my mother and grandmother and God knows who else. All the efforts I had made to keep it together until I got away were to no avail. As I made my way to the airport the next day I felt a mixture of relief and dread. I was beginning another journey, one where the outcome was unknown, undecided. Apart from my brief week in England when I had run away, most of which was spent confined to my dad's pub, I had no knowledge of the place. I was going to my father but that would mean going to his partner and I didn't know how that would work out. I must be the unluckiest girl in the country! First, I got pregnant, then I got pregnant again. I missed out on the chance to work and the opportunity to return to education. I thought I had come up with a fool-proof plan that would at least save my mother the hurt of knowing about my second pregnancy but that plan had hit me in the face. I was so stupid! That sense of being the unluckiest girl in Ireland kicked in even more when I arrived at the departures area in the airport and was met by a sight I could never have imagined.

I thought I was seeing things when I noticed a group of nuns coming towards me. They looked like they were floating, their long habits hiding their feet as they moved as a collective nearer and nearer to me. And who was heading them up? Only the nun who ran Bessborough House. 'This isn't real,' was my first thought. 'How did they find me?' my second. I couldn't believe my eyes. Yet here they were and as she got nearer it was obvious that she recognised me. Oh my God. Were they coming for me? Had they found out I was pregnant again? These thoughts made no sense but when I saw them I was assailed with such an awful feeling of shame, and guilt.

'Hello Margaret,' the nun who had been in charge in Bessborough House took the lead as usual. Even here, she couldn't give me my real name.

'Hello,' I answered hesitantly.

I couldn't stop the thoughts from coming. They knew. She knew. They were here to get me, to stop me and bring me back to the home. The thoughts followed in quick succession, and even though they didn't make any sense, the shame and fear I felt when I saw her made me believe them for an instant. I instinctively wanted to put my hands in front of my stomach to hide it from their penetrating stares. We stood there for only a few minutes, but they seemed to stretch on and on. She was the only one who spoke. The rest of them stood a little bit behind her, a posse waiting to catch me out. I tried to act normal, explaining that I was going over to London to visit my father. Even then, the automatic response to the authority they exuded, the need to explain when I didn't have to, the pretence at politeness when not only was I in total shock to see them turning up there, but also had no time for any of them. 'How is your baby?' she asked.

'She's fine.' In my head I could see that good old Catholic God shaking his finger at me. Aha. You thought you'd get away with it, didn't you? The meeting with them that day really unnerved me and I couldn't shake off the feeling that they knew, because in some divine way they were more powerful than I was. I couldn't wait to get away from them and when I made my excuses, saying I needed to catch my flight, it was as if I was asking permission to leave them. The indoctrination of years of Catholic teaching on their superiority, and my position as the lowly sinner, came home to roost that day.

When I arrived in London and reached the airport arrivals hall I couldn't wait to meet my father. He hugged me and said, 'What have you gotten yourself into?' But it didn't feel like a judgemental comment. I was exhausted, physically and mentally, and for the first time I thought I looked pregnant. It was as if my body was saying, 'Okay, you don't have to pretend any more. You can let it all out now.' All I wanted to do was to get somewhere safe and lie down. All pub managers had living quarters above their premises and we drove back to his flat. I don't know what I expected but it was nothing like the run-down shabby furniture we had been left with when he took off and left us with nothing. It was hard not to feel a jolt of anger and envy when I saw his living conditions. I had a cup of tea and was shown to my room.

As I got undressed and tried to settle myself for the night I wondered how this was going to work out. I would be here for a few months and I didn't know what living with them would be like. I needn't have worried about that though, as I was not going to last long here anyway.

10

'I'm Not Your Daddy!'

'Do you remember
that Wembley front room
with the curry wallpaper
and the ghee yellow kitchen.'

— Rory Duffy, *Wembley High Road*

Taking the boat or plane to England in the 1970s was a rite of passage. Most of my friends ended up there eventually. They went with their boyfriends, or in a group, craving a new experience and different environments, yet inevitably ending up in an Irish gathering, a collective they couldn't seem to be separated from. Numerous songs and poems have been written about the Irish experience in London, songs of life and work, the pubs and music scene, the bedsits and the building sites. Wembley, Cricklewood, Kilburn, Kentish Town and Hampstead became as familiar as the names of any Irish town or village. For many, in spite of being in what appeared as a little Ireland across the water, it was still an exciting experience. Some even chose to remain, making it their home. For me, the trip to England had different connotations. I had joined the ranks of the thousands of pregnant unmarried women who fled to England in order to escape the judgement of a strict, moralistic and intolerant society. The fact that I would be considered a 'second offender' added to that intolerance. So I went to England out of desperation, not a sense of adventure, in order to hide my crime of carrying an illegitimate child for the second time. I didn't really know what to expect over there, but I figured craic would not be high on the agenda. When my friends spoke of their time in England in later years, they would regale us with tales of the people they met, the epic pub brawls they encountered or sometimes even initiated, the great music scene, the drugs, girls, men, work, well, maybe not work, although the ability to earn more money was another aspect of life there. That some of them spent it as quickly as they made it was just part of the fun. I, on the other hand, was hiding out in my father's apartment with the woman he had left home with, the woman he had chosen over his family. Maybe some of my friends' stories were exaggerated, but I too was learning how to stretch the truth. I was hiding out in one of the busiest cities in the world, pretending to everyone back home that I was living the dream in London. I was also witnessing the death of all my fantasies, all I had imagined this time would be like. The first imaginary ideal to die was the one of what it would be like to live with my father again. I don't know what I had expected, but the reality was that I didn't know who this man was any more. He was my father, he still looked the same, but he was not the father I remembered. He was my father when he met me and hugged me tightly in the airport, but he was a different man when we got back to where he lived. He wasn't the man I had grown up with, the man who had sat and laboured over my maths homework with me, or helped me do a jigsaw puzzle. This was a man in a different and relatively new relationship and I had walked right into the middle of this expecting him to be the same, to look after me, when he now had other priorities.

The first few days were awkward, to say the least. I had to pretend to accept and like someone whom I had blamed for taking my father away. I had to remember to speak to him in a different way, not the old familiar way of my childhood. I had to keep my mouth shut. When you are sixteen it's not always easy to see things from the other person's perspective, especially if you have been hurt. My time at Bessborough House had caused me to reflect, and at times I had been less judgemental about my father. Being there made me aware that I wasn't perfect and that we all make mistakes. But it was one thing to know this in my head and quite another to watch him with a woman other than my mother. It was so hard to see him in this light and to realise he was happy here. There had always been a part of me that hoped he would change his mind and return home to us some day. Staying with them now, seeing their familiar domestic routine, brought home to me that there was never going to be any return to life as we had known it. In hindsight, it must have been difficult for them as well. This was the woman that my siblings and I had gone out of our way to make life as difficult as possible for back in Ireland. It must have been hard for her to open her home up to me. When he left home I told all my friends that I would rather he had died. That way I wouldn't have to admit that he had chosen someone else over us, that way he would not have been making a choice to leave us behind. That was what had hurt so much, and beneath all my bravado I was still that hurt and angry young girl. But I couldn't let any of this show. I needed their help and I would have to play happy families with them until my baby arrived, even as I harboured such volatile and confusing emotions and thoughts towards them. And God only knows what thoughts and feelings they had about me and my presence there. Looking back, going over there was probably not the best of ideas, but I didn't feel that I had any other choice. So we were stuck with each other and I now had to decide what I was going to do next. I don't remember sitting down to discuss options with anyone. It's as if adoption were the unspoken consensus, even though it was not what I wanted. I hadn't thought any of this through. I had been in such a panic to get away, to make sure no one found out I was pregnant again, that I hadn't taken the time to think about how this would work out.

Something happened one evening that brought the reality of my situation home to me with a shock. I had gone downstairs to the bar area to ask if I could get some crisps. I usually spent my time upstairs in the flat, away from the public. My father was chatting to someone at the bar. 'Can I get a packet of crisps, Daddy?' I said.

He turned and looked at me and I knew I had done something wrong. 'Sure,' he said, excusing himself from his conversation and following me back up the stairs. He went mad! 'I told you not to call me that.' He had asked me not to call him Daddy in public, to use his given name, but I had not realised the ramifications of doing so and had called him Daddy without thinking. He was my father, after all. The bottom line was, that as far as anyone knew, he was married to this other woman. The company he worked for required that the couples running the pub be married, and as divorce was illegal in Ireland they just pretended to be married. There was no room for me or my siblings in this arrangement. He was not my daddy over here and I needed to remember that.

Whoa, when did that happen? I don't remember any wedding. He's still legally married to my mother.

I'm pretty sure he had not factored in any visits from me or my siblings when he came up with this plan. It was a double whammy. A whole other level of abandonment. It really shook me, but I knew that if I wanted to stay in England, if I wanted help in dealing with this pregnancy, I would have to continue to pretend not to be his daughter in public. He would help me, but it would be on his terms. I couldn't even argue about it. This was another form of silencing, different from what I had experienced in Bessborough, but a silencing nevertheless. My time here would be an emotional minefield. Initially I had thought that it was uncomfortable because she didn't want me there, and there may even have been some truth in that, but the reality was my being there made life very uncomfortable for both of them. I quickly began to realise that if it wasn't for me being pregnant and needing help there is no way he would ever have invited me over to stay with him.

One evening my father asked me if I would like to go to bingo with her. I had such a feeling of déjà vu. Remember the day trip to Dublin? I didn't feel as if I had a choice, and maybe it was their way of trying to reach out to me and involving me in their lives. It also meant having some time away from the restrictions of the apartment. I had no interest in bingo. Back home it was a pastime for a lot of the women who lived on our road but my mother had never had an interest in the game and it wasn't something we had been introduced to. I got myself ready and we left. I can't remember how she passed me off, who she introduced me as, but my one prevailing memory of that night was the bacon sandwiches, which were delicious. What can I say? I was sixteen and pregnant. Other than that evening there were not too many forays outside, and while my friends worked and played in rooms with 'curry wallpaper' and yellow kitchens, I kept close to the place I called home for now. Strangely enough, the straw that broke the camel's back was not the day I innocently called my father by his proper title, but the evening when I insisted on ironing his shirts. Now, this was probably the most ridiculous thing I could have suggested doing. Back at home, even with a daughter of my own, I was almost forbidden from looking in the hot press, never mind ironing the clothes that went in there. But I was offering to iron his shirts for work, in order to prove myself useful. I felt like I was a burden to everyone and was probably operating from a mixture of 'you owe me but I don't deserve help, so I'll offer to help you instead'. When I saw the pile of shirts I felt very much out of my depth, but I valiantly carried on, ironing them as I was instructed and hanging them up on hangers. Later on I was informed that they were a disgrace and it was unbelievable that someone my age didn't know how to iron shirts.

Shortly after that my father told me there wasn't enough room there to be comfortable and that they had decided it would be better if I moved to the home of her daughter, who also ran a pub with her husband. They had a family and I would probably be more comfortable there. I could help out with the boys too. I didn't protest. What would have been the point? I had no voice here either. I was a problem and nothing else. And this had nothing to do with my lack of ironing skills. We would never have survived living together. I needed my father's help but I was not ready to forgive either of them. This would not happen until years later. So I packed up my belongings and my father drove me over to meet the family I would be staying with until my baby was born. I wasn't wanted by him so I found it hard to believe at first that I would be wanted by his partner's daughter. But eventually I settled into their home and from the first time I met her all she ever did was treat me with kindness. Maybe it was because she was younger and had children, maybe it was because of her own life experience or maybe she was just a kind person. But it was good to have someone that I could talk to and ask questions of. She helped me feel comfortable in their home and I could talk to her about my pregnancy and the options available to me. I seemed to spend a lot of time waiting, waiting for letters from home, waiting for my antenatal appointments, waiting for support in making a decision about this pregnancy. Waiting, waiting, waiting. Running a pub is hard work and this woman and her husband were busy, but she made time to show me around the local area, pointing out the best market stalls and boutiques and making sure I knew my way around and wouldn't get lost if I ventured out on my own. I knew there were people from home in London at the time and I prayed I wouldn't bump into any of them. They would be enjoying the city and I wished I could do so also, but I had a different reason for being here. The woman

I was staying with often brought me with her when she went shopping. I loved those times when I could walk alongside her and her children and feel like part of someone's family. She loved her style and often asked my opinion when she was buying something new. I wished I was as confident and sophisticated as she was. It's funny, but to this day I cannot remember the name of the pub they ran but I can remember strolling across Westminster Bridge and walking through the iconic shopping streets. She also helped me to organise my antenatal appointments in Guy's Hospital and to get to my first meeting with a support worker to discuss the options open to me as a young unmarried mother from Ireland. One day she announced that as it was such a lovely day we should make a trip to the seaside. We travelled by train and spent the day wandering around the market stalls and walking along the beach. I wished I could go swimming but I didn't have a suit with me and I would probably have been too conscious of how I looked. It might not have been up there with the way my friends experienced London, but don't forget that the previous year I had spent seven months locked away in a mother and baby home, so a train trip to the beach was a definite improvement.

As far as my friends and most of my family were concerned, I was living the life of the Irish emigrant, working and having a great time in London. Some probably even thought that I was very selfish, heading off to London and leaving my mother to look after her granddaughter. But while it wasn't anything like being in Bessborough House I still felt as trapped as I had back then. The walks to the city, the trips to the seaside and the odd shopping excursion with my father were welcome distractions, and on those occasions he would give me money to buy clothes that I sent home for my daughter. Shopping in London should have been such a treat. We didn't have large shopping centres at home and I was mesmerised by the abundance of style on display. It was the same when we went on a day trip to the beach – lines and lines of outdoor stalls selling cheesecloth tops and leather goods. A teenager's paradise, if one weren't in hiding, pregnant. Apart from this, one day morphed into the next, with the exception of one particular day. We had just entered Marks & Spencer when a voice over the tannoy announced that everyone should leave the store in a quiet and orderly manner. I didn't realise it at first but there was a bomb scare. The nearest I had been to a bomb scare was watching clips on a television screen. She was used to this and calmly organised for us to leave. But I was afraid. I was heavily pregnant and I can remember trying to ignore the urge to run out the doors of the store. I was also aware of her nervous energy beneath her calm manner. Up to this I had not given much thought to what it was like for people who lived with this threat daily or what it was like to be Irish in London during these years. Other than that, the only thing that changed that summer was my size, and the fact that I was now regularly seeing a support worker from an adoption agency.

I was facing the hardest decision I would ever have to make in my life. No matter what way I looked at it, it seemed impossible that I would be able to keep this baby. I wrote home to my mother and told her how I was getting on. At least I didn't have to pretend to her that I was working over here. I also told her my due date and any comments the clinic made, but these comments were never acknowledged in her return letters. While it seemed as if I was being supported by my family, it was made abundantly clear that I would not be keeping this baby. Eventually I would have to make a decision.

When I went to my first appointment with the adoption agency the woman I was staying with came with me. It was the same with my first appointment in Guy's Hospital. Once I became familiar with the different routes I went to my appointments alone. I would then take the time to explore the city a little, but I was always encouraged not to stay away for too long, to get home in time for the evening meal or just get home. My support worker was very good. She listened, explained the various options and gave me time to think about what I wanted to do. If I decided to go down the route of adoption, and there didn't really seem to be another option for me, she would help me through the whole process. I would have a certain amount of autonomy, which didn't happen in Ireland. When I felt my baby move for the first time it really brought it home to me that this was not going to be easy. When I had been in Bessborough House the previous year I was adamant that I was keeping my baby, and that resolution became even stronger when I felt the first movements. After that there was no going back for me. This time would be different. Abortion had never been on the table for me, though it was legal in England at this time. It would have been too late and I was too indoctrinated in Catholicism to go ahead with it even if it hadn't been. But I was also indoctrinated enough to know that if I went down the route of adoption I didn't want my child in a Catholic home and I didn't want to work with a Catholic agency. Bessborough House had been enough for me and I didn't want my child to have any affiliation with a Catholic institution, or to go to a Catholic home, for that matter. When I went to meet my support worker we would discuss how I was getting on and how my pregnancy was progressing. I was asked my opinion about what type of family I would ideally like my child to grow up in. What was important to me? Financial security, education, class, religion, other family members? This made me feel that I had some agency over where my baby would grow up. Imagine having to decide these things at sixteen. I was a mother already, but not in the true sense of the word, not when it came to making such life-defining decisions for another person. These discussions also made me aware of how powerless we had been in Bessborough House, where children were taken away and the mothers had no idea where they had ended up. In England I never felt that I was pressurised and I went to these appointments regularly, where files on applicants for adoption were produced and discussed. It was as if I was outside of myself, watching someone else having these conversations. I often thought that it would never come to this anyway. Yes, I would work with the agency. Yes, I would discuss the files on the different applicants and think about what I wanted for my child, but deep down inside I still held on to some small scrap of belief that even one of my parents would relent and that I would either be allowed to bring my second child back to Ireland or I would return home to collect my daughter and we would all live in London. If that happened I would have to tell her father that he had a second child, but I would cross that bridge when I came to it. I felt as if I had a choice, a certain level of autonomy in deciding which family my child would go to, but in reality I had even less choice than I had when I was pregnant the year before. In the end I was planning to do what the nuns in Bessborough hadn't been able to make me do. I had far more freedom than I had had in Bessborough, but the prison gates of Irish society were as secure as they had been then and I couldn't go home. So I kept my appointments with the agency and the hospital, spent time with the family I was staying with and waited to go into labour. And all the time I prayed for some sort of miracle that would change things.

Between myself and my support worker we had narrowed down the search for adoptive parents to two couples. I was drawn to one, which seems strange, as I would not be meeting them until after the birth of my baby, and only if I chose to hand over my child myself, something I had the option to do but wasn't sure about yet. It seemed like an impossible thing to imagine and I was still harbouring secret thoughts that things might go differently and I could bring my baby home. I had no idea how I would manage that either. How would we survive in a house with my mother and siblings? Would I be able to go back to work? Was it fair to expect my mother to help me with two children? No matter what way I looked at it, there seemed to be no way out.

At my final appointment with the hospital near the end of September they decided that if I didn't go into labour by the next appointment they would bring me in and induce me. I didn't know what this involved. I hoped it didn't mean getting an enema. I had also missed my daughter's first birthday. How would I ever explain that or make up for it? I informed the support worker that my baby would possibly be here some time the following week. All I could think of now was having my baby and getting home as soon as I could. I didn't want to think about the in-between part, the handing over. Start again, that was the plan. Put the last two years behind me. Never get involved with a man again and make some sort of life for myself and my baby girl. On 7 October 1974 I went into Guy's Hospital to prepare for the birth. I was nervous, but not as nervous as I had been in Bessborough. At least I had some idea of what to expect. I had everything I needed. One thing my father didn't scrimp on was getting me everything I would need for this baby. I was prepared. But this birth would not be anything like my daughter's and I wasn't prepared for the reality of seeing my baby and then having to let him or her go.

11

'Shut Her Up!'

'Silence is expected.'

– Sarah Ahmed, *Living a Feminist Life*

The medical staff arrived at my bed early in the morning. It was decided that nature needed a little nudge and they were going to induce my labour. I didn't know what this meant, but I was grateful to be in a proper hospital with qualified staff around in case anything went wrong. I was probably a little over-confident also. I mean, I had given birth in Bessborough House and if I had managed that I couldn't see a problem here. The nurses were efficient but kind and I didn't feel the same judgement or punishment that I had felt in Cork. Some of the other women in the ward had already given birth, and some were waiting to have their babies. I assumed they were all married and would be going home with their newborn babies. Then again, as far as I knew, none of them knew anything about my circumstances, so how could I know the truth of theirs? The nurses would have known that I was one of the Irish girls over here to have her baby, then go back home as if nothing had happened. They may have discussed this among themselves but I didn't think they could talk about in the ward. Yes, this was a safe, secure, confidential place and I was glad of that. The ward was quiet and organised, or as quiet as a ward with babies in it could be. The sister in charge seemed to run a tight ship and maintained a well-ordered routine. You could see how the manner and body language of the staff changed when she appeared and this filtered down to us, the patients in the ward. No one ever questioned anything she said. She seemed nice but it was obvious that she ruled with an iron fist.

In the evenings the quiet was broken with the arrival of visiting hours. On my first evening there I felt that I stood out as the women in the other beds all seemed to have visitors while I had none. No one thought of coming to visit me that evening. They thought I would need the rest before I had my baby. I thought that evening marked me out, highlighting that my situation was different from that of the other women in the ward. I pretended to read my book while, out of the corner of my eye, I watched the other women open presents for their new babies, or offer around the biscuits or fruit that had been given to them. I watched them chat easily with their friends and families and I felt very isolated. I worried that this would be the same after my baby was born, but after the first day I usually had someone come to see me either in the late afternoon or the evening. My father and the woman I was staying with came to visit and my support worker from the adoption agency came to see how I was getting on. I didn't want to see her, not because I didn't like her, but because it reminded me that time was short. Her reason for visiting was to see how I was but also to prepare me for the handing over of my baby. The inevitability of having my child adopted had emerged slowly over the course of the last couple of months. I had the option of not seeing him or her after the birth, going back to the ward to recuperate and going home when I was ready, or I could spend the time with my child and then do the handover myself. I had decided on the latter option. I didn't think I could just leave my baby in the labour ward and pretend she or he didn't exist. I was told that I could change my mind at any time, but I felt that it was the least I could do for my child. That first night was lonely, but tomorrow I would see my baby. I sorted out my belongings and tried to settle down for the night. I didn't think any further than the following morning or what would happen after that.

Early the next morning I was examined again and a drip was attached to my arm. Some of the women in the ward offered words of encouragement and support. 'They are very good here.' 'This is my second and they are great.' 'It will all be behind you soon.' I didn't tell them that I knew what to expect, that I had already had one child. I imagine they wanted to put my mind at rest as I was so young. I was not in any pain or discomfort at the moment so I lay back and tried to read or listen to the radio. There were headphones attached to the arm of the bed and we could listen to the radio though these. This was such a novelty. There was nothing like this when I was in hospital in Ireland and the choice of music was so much better here than at home, where the only access to the latest pop music was when I listened to Radio Luxembourg on my transistor under the sheets late at night. Here I could choose from a number of stations and listen to the latest top chart music. It sounds mad now that I was even interested in listening to pop music or could be so entertained by the novelty of the headphones, but I was sixteen and at times I wanted to pretend none of this was happening to me. So I spent my day on the headphones, or reading. I went for an occasional stroll down the long stretch of the ward, or went to the bathroom, hauling my drip behind me. In the afternoon I began to feel the first pangs, not too strong, but strong enough for me to recognise that my labour would soon begin in earnest. It would not be long now. When the nurse came back to see how I was getting on I let her know and she went off to get someone. 'What will they do now?' I wondered. Hopefully it would not include an enema and I was pretty sure I would have proper pain relief. This would not be like Cork. Sure enough, no one made me do anything more than walk around a bit, which was fine with me. Other than that they seemed happy to just keep an eye on me and wait until I was ready to go to the labour ward.

I was nervous but I was also looking forward to being on the other side of this, to seeing and holding my baby. I knew I would not be bringing my baby home but I still wanted to meet him or her. I didn't mind whether it was a boy or a girl as long as the baby was healthy. As they wheeled me down to the labour ward I thought to myself that at least I knew what to expect here. I was surprised to see a group of people standing around the labour bed. In Bessborough it was a midwife and a girl from the house who helped me deliver my baby, but here it looked like a whole team of people. I was helped to scoot onto the bed, no climbing up on your own here. That was good. I felt a sharp prick of a needle and remember thinking that they were not going to make me suffer here as they had in Cork. 'This will help you relax and help with the pain,' one of the team said. I don't know what they gave me but this was the polar opposite of my experience in Bessborough. I felt like I was drugged out of my head. I kept drifting off, then coming to with the realisation that there were people working on my body. When this happened I would try to ask where my baby was and what was happening to me. But it came out like garbled shouts and groans, like shouting out in the middle of a nightmare. I could hear voices and thought I heard someone saying, 'Shut that bitch up,' but I was so out of it that I couldn't say if it was real or not. Later, I definitely heard someone again saying, 'Just shut her up.' What was happening? Again, all control had been taken out of my hands. I could have had my baby naturally. God knows, it couldn't have been more natural in Cork. I had no say here either, and if they had explained what they were going to do I probably wouldn't have had the confidence to argue with them. Just like in Bessborough House, when it came to it, as a young pregnant woman I had no say in what was happening to me, no voice. When I was having my daughter in Bessborough I had been fully aware of everything that was happening and even though I thought they were cruel and uncaring, I saw her being born, I witnessed her arrival. I was involved in the process. I had thought that here I would have that same involvement but I was so sedated that I didn't know what was happening. Every time I came to I thought my baby had died and I began to panic and try to sit up, asking them what was happening. But it seemed as if I was just a nuisance to them, someone emitting garbled shouts and groans, someone who should shut up and let them get on with it. This was even worse than Bessborough. I felt that I had nothing to do with this child they were delivering, and that I was doing something wrong, that I was an inconvenience and someone not deserving of the full birth experience. Maybe that is the way it was for everyone in a hospital setting back then. I don't know, but in 1978, when my first son from my marriage was born, it was nothing like this, and that was just a few years short years later. It was a natural birth and I felt that I was fully present to greet him. But this was a nightmare and I felt angry, hurt and judged by the whole thing. I can't even remember seeing my son when he was born. I was so out of it, so disconnected from the process that it was the next day before I remembered anything. Was this a punishment for being pregnant and not married, for committing the cardinal sin of getting pregnant twice outside of marriage? For being a 'second offender'? These were probably not rational thoughts. I had believed that unmarried mothers were treated differently in England but now I was not so sure.

After what I can only describe as the trauma of his birth, I spent the following week looking after my son. I had decided that I wanted to spend the time with him. If a week was all that I could give him, I wanted it to be a week that would mean something. He was perfect. Ten perfect little fingers, ten perfect little toes, and he looked so like his sister in Ireland. It was heartbreaking. I wrote to my mother and told her all about him, what he had weighed, how much like his sister he looked and how perfect he was. I told her how I was and that I was recovering well from the birth. I didn't go into anything about what a nightmare the labour had been, just focused on telling her all about her new grandson. When she replied she never referred to the birth or to my son. She told me how my daughter was getting on, filled me in on the local news and asked when I would be returning home. Whatever tiny bit of hope I had about her changing her mind and allowing me come home with him was shattered when I received her letter. It was the same when my father visited. He looked at his grandson and smiled. 'He is perfect,' he said, but there was never any mention of finding a way to keep him with us. I was told many years later that the whole episode had broken his heart, but that was cold comfort and I didn't see any sign of that during the days I spent in the hospital. I had named him after my father but that didn't make any difference either. I tried to make the most of every day I spent with him, ignoring the fact that the day of handing him over to his new family was getting closer and closer. I told him how much I loved him and that he had a sister at home in Ireland. I told him about his father's family as well and, most of all, I told him that I wanted the best for him and that he was going to have a life that I could never have given him in Ireland. I told him how sorry I was and asked him to forgive me. I talked to him, sang to him, bathed him and changed his nappies and I hugged him close to me. I didn't have him at night as the babies were looked after by the nursing staff then. This was to give the new mothers an opportunity to get some rest before they went home. If one of the babies didn't settle the mother would be woken up and brought to the nursery to tend to her baby. Most nights the ward would be quiet and peaceful. But I spent as much time with him during the day as I could.

In a way the maternity ward in Guy's Hospital was a sort of cocoon, a place to spend time with my son, uninterrupted except for the odd visitor or the arrival of my support worker. Whenever she arrived she brought a rush of reality with her and I had to face the fact that this time would not last. Every day at 2.00 p.m. the ward sister would arrive, dim all the lights and ask us to lie on our stomachs and rest. I say asked, but as she patrolled the ward checking to see that we were all lying in the correct position, it was more like being ordered to do so. She was like a sergeant major inspecting the troops, but in hindsight it was a good idea and ensured the women in the ward had some quiet time. I'm not sure what the idea of lying on the stomach was, but I found it very relaxing. After this quiet time we would prepare for our visitors. It probably shouldn't have come as such a shock; after all Ireland is never far away and it is a small world, but I still couldn't believe it when I looked up one day saw my aunt, who lived in Athlone, walking through the ward, looking directly at me as I sat with my son.

What the hell is she doing here, was my first panicky thought. How did she know? This was mad.

'What are you doing here?' I asked.

'I came over to visit your father and I was wondering where you were. I wanted to see how you were getting on. He told me you were here.'

I found that hard to believe. She had just happened to visit my father, in London, while I just happened to be here, pregnant.

Jesus Christ, there's no getting away from any of ye, I thought.

That was when I began to realise that he must have told all of them. There was no way that first my grandmother guessed and now my aunt. As if I hadn't enough to deal with. I didn't want her there. I didn't want any of them there. I just wanted to spend time with my son before I had to let him go. What a mess! I can't remember what we spoke about, whether we made small talk or whether she wanted to know all about how I had ended up here. I felt like an exhibit. Did all the staff know who she was? The next time my father came to visit I read him the riot act. It was none of their business and I was raging to think that he would have told his family. He said at the time that he hadn't, that she had come over on an unexpected visit and was asking about where I was. He had no choice but to tell her. I didn't believe him. My time with my son was so short and so precious and this intrusion into that time felt invasive. Even though she had not said anything awful to me, her visit brought the sense of judgement from home into the room. I felt trapped the day she walked in. I had nowhere to hide and the fact that I had even had that thought reminded me again of how shameful all of this was, as if I had done something terrible. Thank God she had to go back home before I had my last day with my son. That was something I didn't want to share with any of my family.

The day before I was due to meet his adoptive family and hand him over to them, my support worker came to see me. She wanted to make sure I was okay and to see if I needed her to come with me when I met them. I had already decided that this was something I wanted to do myself. I knew she would be there, waiting for me when I came out of the meeting room. I don't know why I felt so strongly about this, about spending the week with him, or personally handing him over to them. I think part of it was that I was the one responsible, it was my fault that I couldn't bring him home with me. I realise now that this irrational need to take full responsibility was something I had inherited from the Church teaching I had grown up with and from my time in Bessborough. It was the collective ideal of a suppressed society that was dictated to by the Church and it fed into the idea that the woman was at fault. It was Eve who did it, it was the woman who was responsible. Regardless of the whys, though, I do not regret spending that week with my son, or the decision to meet his new parents. If I had nothing else, I would have the memories of that week, the joys and the pain, the love and the loss. I would know that I had handed him over safely and with love. I also had no idea how traumatic this meeting would be. I had never met these people before. Sure, I had read an outline of their lives, how they made their living, their religion, their standing in their community, but I didn't know them and I was blindly trusting them to love my son, to give him what I couldn't give him, to be a mother and father to him. I prayed I was making the right decision, but there was no alternative for me at this stage.

This was the day. The day to say a final goodbye. I was also going home, well, home to the family I had stayed with throughout my pregnancy. I packed my bag and dressed carefully. I wanted to make a good impression. I fed and dressed my son and wrapped him in a baby blanket. I had already noticed his little quirks, which side he liked best when feeding, how he liked to be held. I could tell her all of this. I wasn't thinking of the fact that they would make their own rituals, their own ways of being together. When the time came my support worker was there, but my son and I went into the room alone to meet his new family. It is so hard even to write this down, to try to remember while not wanting to. In a way it sometimes feels as if I am talking about someone else, some other girl this happened to. And I am afraid. Afraid that if I get too close to the memories I will crumble and lose myself totally in them. So maybe it is better to write from a distance of time, with the slight numbness that that confers. If I can't feel it, it won't hurt as much. I know that both parents and their son were there in the room. I can see them sitting there, but I can't see their faces. I can remember talking to them, but I can't hear their voices. What I can remember are images and feelings, the weight of him in my arms as I entered the room and the emptiness when I left it, the awareness that I couldn't touch this feeling or I would fall apart. I know they were so happy to meet him and so grateful for him. I know they didn't rush me, and I held on to him for most of the meeting. 'Please tell him about me.' 'Please tell him I loved him so much.' 'Please explain to him why I couldn't keep him.' 'Please let him keep his name, the name I have given him.' 'Please tell him he has a sister.' They said yes to everything I asked of them. And when it couldn't be put off any longer I kissed him, smelled his unique baby smell for the last time and handed him over. She took him as if I had given her the crown jewels and I had a fleeting sense that I had made the right choice, that she would love him as much as I did. Then I left the room. I couldn't bear to be there for another moment. My support worker was outside waiting for me. I know there is a lot of talk these days about agencies and how awful some of them were, but she was so kind, and genuinely wanted to make sure I was okay. My father was waiting to bring me home. I held back the tears until I got into the car. I sobbed the whole way home and went straight to my room when we arrived at the apartment. I couldn't bear to talk to anyone. I just wanted to be left alone with my sorrow. How was I going to get through this? I wanted to pack everything and just get out of there. I wanted to go home. I wanted to see my daughter. But I couldn't leave yet. I needed another few days to recover from the birth and I also needed to sign the interim adoption papers before I left.

I can't explain how I felt on that day, or the days to come. I was numb inside. It was as if what was happening was too big to put a name to. I wanted to go home, but I didn't. I wanted to change my mind and keep my son, but I felt I couldn't. I moped around the place and tried to act as if I was okay, but I wasn't fooling anyone. My father thought that once I got home and began the rest of my life things would sort themselves out. I don't know if he believed that but both he and I knew that when I got home

I would be living a life of pretence. I couldn't tell anyone about my son. At that time I had no idea what this suppression would cost me, emotionally and psychologically. When the day came to sign the final forms I went on my own. I had been asked if I wanted photographs or reports of how my son was getting on but I said no. I don't know if the family he was with would have stuck to this if I had said yes, but I didn't think I could bear to see him or know how he was doing, not when I couldn't keep him with me. I believed at the time that a clean break was the best. This is one of my biggest regrets now. When I arrived back at the apartment I went straight to my room. I lay for hours staring at the ceiling. I was just numb, there is no other word I can think of to describe how I felt. The woman I was staying with came in two or three times to check on me but I ignored her. When she finally called me to have something to eat, she said that I must have been exhausted as I had slept for the whole afternoon. But I had not been asleep. I had been wide awake. I had seen her coming in. 'No,' she said, 'I checked several times and you were fast asleep.' I knew I wasn't. I thought I must have been in some altered state of consciousness because I could see and hear her but as far as she was concerned I was asleep. Back then I didn't recognise trauma for what it was. When the day came for me to fly home my father brought me to the airport. I had a case full of trendy clothes, presents for my daughter and everyone else at home. I was the emigrant daughter returning home from the big city of London, even though I had only been there for a short time. I had my story straight. In reality I had travelled to a different land altogether. It was the last time I set foot in London.

12

Returning Emigrant

'Grief is different. Grief has no distance. Grief comes in waves.'
– Joan Didion, *The Year of Magical Thinking*

I don't have clear memories of my arrival home from England. My father booked a flight for me but I can't remember arriving in Dublin Airport or how I made my way home to Athlone. It's as if my mind had enough things to cope with, things like the trauma of my son's birth, the smell and feel of him in my arms, the emptiness I felt after I left him. The mundane memories of coming home and finding where I fit in again took second place. So I don't have step-by-step images of how I finally got home, who picked me up or how I got back to Athlone. I can remember my father pouring a brandy for me before I left his pub for the last time. It was to calm my nerves before the flight. I drank it in one go and he looked shocked. 'You're supposed to sip it,' he said. But he had not gone through the week I had gone through. I remember wishing I could have another one when I was sitting on the plane waiting for it to take off. Wishing I had something to take the edge off. That feeling would become a familiar one in the years to come and I know there were times when I used alcohol or drugs to push down the feelings of desperation, fear and guilt that followed me around as I tried to get my life back, tried to find some kind of equilibrium. This arrival home was very different from my arrival home from Bessborough. There was no welcoming committee this time, no good wishes for a baby no one knew anything about, no excitement when I walked through the front gate.

I had turned seventeen the week after my son was born, but there were no birthday celebrations in England. As my friends didn't know what had happened while I was away they were keen to know what I had done and what we would do now to celebrate belatedly. What did I tell them? What stories did I make up to convince them that I had had a good time while I was away? I can't remember. I'm sure the fact that my father ran a pub came in handy when I talked about my night life. Trauma impacts us in many different ways and I believe my lack of memory regarding those first few days at home is partly due to everything that happened and partly due to the immediate need to pretend nothing had happened. What is it they say about lying? Tell yourself the lie for long enough and you eventually come to believe it. I don't know how true that is, as I never forgot about my son or the events of that summer in England, but the need to push it down became easier as the months and years progressed. There was no one I could talk to anyway, no one I could tell, so I had to get on with things.

Being reunited with my daughter made this a little easier. I had missed her first birthday and wanted to make up for this. From now on there would be no more crises, no more need to leave her. I was determined to find a job, begin to contribute to the household and build some sort of a life. I was only seventeen. It was not too late. When I returned from Bessborough House I had applied for the Unmarried Mother's Allowance. I had signed this over to my mother and I also contributed part of my wages before I went to England. She had looked after my daughter while I was away and now I wanted to make up for that. There was a position going in the shop I had worked in before I left for England. I felt uncomfortable approaching them, especially as I had turned down their offer of help in going back to school, but I took the bull by the horns one day and went to talk to them. They were happy to give me my old position back and I felt that things might work out for once.

Life returned to normal. You would never think I had had a baby or left a baby behind. It was never mentioned again, even up to my parents' deaths. The only remark my mother ever made about that time was that there were 'girls like you' who liked 'that sort of thing', and I had better be careful. That, along with the advice that no one would want someone who already had a child. Her ideas of sex and sexuality were mired in the teachings of the Church, filtered through the lens of sin and immorality. It wasn't that she didn't love me or care for me, but she really believed my soul was in danger of eternal hell and she thought she was giving me sound advice. I believe this thinking filtered down to me unconsciously, resulting in episodes of uncontrollable fits of guilt and remorse. I thought I had a more modern and liberal approach to life, but my reaction when I went for my final out-patient's appointment at Guy's Hospital shows the strength of the religious system I grew up in and how that message of shame and sin had taken hold, even if unconsciously. Before I left the hospital that day, I was asked if I wanted any advice about birth control. My instinctive reaction was one of indignation. What kind of a girl did they think I was? Did they think I would go home and get pregnant again straight away? Did they think I couldn't control myself? 'No, thank you,' I said, adding to myself, 'I'm not like that, you know.' It's hard to explain, but it is as if one part of me knew that I wasn't a bad person, while another part of me felt guilty all the time, as if I had done something horrible and had to defend myself constantly. This skewed way of thinking, this irrational need to defend myself, when they were only offering advice that I would not have had access to back in Ireland, shows the extent to which I had internalised the message of the Catholic Church regarding women and their sexual lives and how damaging this message was. You were either the virtuous woman or the sinful one, you kept yourself pure or you 'liked that sort of thing'. It would take me years to get over this thinking, to realise that I hadn't got pregnant on my own and there was absolutely nothing wrong with me. My ideas about sex were mixed up with shame and guilt, and this burden of shame and guilt fell solely on the woman. It was emblematic of the virgin/whore dichotomy that was fed to us through religion and education and carried on in the family mores. I knew that most of my friends were having sex, but none of them got pregnant, at least not to my knowledge. I had managed to get pregnant twice so I must be really bad. Although I didn't really believe this there was a part of me that took it on board unconsciously.

Things may have seemed normal on the outside, but on the inside I was broken in a million different ways, and had no way of figuring out how I felt, never mind coming to terms with my loss. Both of my parents had let me down and I ended up being the one who felt responsible in some way.

I didn't even speak of my father's rejection that evening in his pub until years later. I painted on a smile and got on with it. 'Just get on with the rest of your life.' That was the mantra, and, as I was supposed to have been over in England working and enjoying the social life there, I couldn't be seen to mope around. So I went back to the old coping mechanisms that had served me so well but that wouldn't quite cut it this time. My mother's words had reminded me that there was something wrong with me and that the chances of meeting someone or getting married were very slim. What was 'the rest of my life' going to look like? Did it mean living in her house, with no hope of ever meeting anyone or getting married, with no road map for the rest of my life? My friends, even the ones who would eventually travel to England and live in squats and have mad adventures, had their Leaving Certs or a typing and shorthand diploma to fall back on. My life, in comparison, looked pretty hopeless. Yet, in spite of all of this, something inside me knew I had made the right decision in not getting married. I would be my own person, whatever that was.

My daughter had grown very close to my mother while I was away. I felt a bit put out by that but I couldn't say anything. My mother had looked after her while I had been away and now I would need to get that relationship back on track. As the job was only up the road from my house I could look after my daughter in the mornings and then walk up to work. I was home again for my lunch break and again in the evenings when I finished. The money helped and before long it was as if I had never been away. At first I found it hard to settle back in and I didn't go out too much. I wanted to prove that I was good, that I could do this, but eventually I began to go out more. My friends had not understood why I was not socialising as much. I was seventeen. Surely my mother would babysit and I could go out occasionally? They had no idea of what I had gone through. None of my siblings had any idea either, so it seemed strange that I did not want to socialise. Eventually I even went out with someone for a while, but it didn't last long. However, it put paid to the idea that no one would ever want me.

Ireland was changing, and while the changes may not have been radical, they were slow but sure. I think people were beginning to wake up, to challenge the restrictive ways of thinking. The introduction of the Unmarried Mother's Allowance in 1973, though the name of the payment is jarring, began to show a change in attitude. And even though the term 'illegitimacy' would not be abolished until 1987, there was already talk about addressing this and ensuring that children born outside of marriage would have equal succession rights. Things were changing, albeit slowly. The plan when I came home was to find some quality of life for me and my daughter, but in reality the longer we were there the more we fell into a pattern of being looked after by my mother. This is not to say that I didn't look after my daughter and do my bit, but my mother took over more and more of her care, and I allowed this to happen. She also watched everything I did, who I met, where I went, what time I came home. As I was seventeen this was normal, but there was always the added suggestion that I couldn't be trusted not to go off the rails, have sex with someone and get pregnant. It never occurred to her to recognise that I didn't ever have random partners, I had had one serious boyfriend who was the father of both of my children and I wasn't in the habit of sleeping around. I think in hindsight the biggest sin in Ireland was that of exposure. It was okay to do what you wanted as long as no one knew, especially the neighbours. God forbid that anyone would find out, and having a baby was like taking out a full-page advertisement in the local paper. Look at what she did! No blame ever attached to the father. I got up every morning and looked after my daughter, went to work, spent some evenings at home and slept with her beside me. I also went out, met friends for a drink or went dancing. My life was normal, but underneath I was a churning mass of unresolved issues and sometimes the unfairness of it all would hit me. But then I would think of how lucky I had been in being able to keep my daughter, to bring her home, to have support, a job and a home for both of us.

Eventually I did meet someone, someone who got to know my daughter and accepted both of us. By this time I had started having my own life. I still looked after my daughter but there was no shortage of babysitters as everyone loved her. Her father, who had left Ireland at this stage, came back to Athlone to see his daughter regularly. He knew my new boyfriend and we often ended up in the same company. In such a small town it would have been impossible to avoid each other anyway. I had wondered if this would be awkward but it didn't seem to be and I thought it was good that we could remain friends and were able to talk to each other. Society was definitely changing – even after I was married my daughter's father would often call to our flat to visit when he was home and sometimes join us for a drink in the evening. I can remember on one occasion when an uncle of mine met us out one evening. He greeted us and chatted for a few minutes, but when he got home he gave out stink, saying we were a disgrace, wondering how the three of us could spend time together as if it was the most normal thing in the world. I thought it was better than everyone fighting and not talking.

My daughter was around four years of age at this stage and from the beginning she had been told who her parents were. My mother didn't agree with this and wanted me to tell her that this man who visited her was a special friend. 'How pervy is that?' I replied. No, if there was one thing I was going to do it was make sure she knew who her parents were; there would be no 'white lies' told in that regard. There was enough lying when I was packed off to Bessborough and again when I went to England. Before we got married I had enrolled for a typing and shorthand course. I was really grateful for the job in the shop, but I wanted to do something more with my life and this was the first step. Back then typing and shorthand were the things that would get you work. I never fully mastered the shorthand but I did develop good typing skills. Getting married was a big step. Our relationship was serious, but in hindsight I was still too young and I hadn't dealt with anything that had happened to me, so it probably was not the wisest decision to make. My positive response to his proposal was mixed with fear. I did love him, but I thought that perhaps no one would ever ask me again. Maybe this was my last chance. This was a crazy way for a nineteen-year-old to be thinking, but then again, maybe it was normal after everything I had experienced. Why we didn't just live together is beyond me, but I was still dogged by that label of 'bad girl' and wanted to do it right. At least this time my mother would have a wedding before there were any other children. Before we got married I told my fiancé about my trip to England and about my son. I told him I would understand if he wanted to call everything off. I felt this was too important to keep from him. I knew this would make or break us and that I was taking a huge risk as he was friends with my son's father. But he understood and he kept the secret safe for me. He was the only person I had told about this at that time.

After our wedding I applied for a job in a local factory. I never thought of returning to education again. As far as I was concerned that ship had sailed. In 1973, while I was still in Bessborough House, the government abolished the compulsory passing of Irish in order to pass a State exam. Shortly after returning home from Bessborough House with my daughter two nuns from the secondary school I had attended arrived to the door. It was déjà vu. Another representative from the Church with another message. One of them was the head sister of the school and she had been very insistent on calling personally to let me know about the change in my exam status, telling me that I had not failed the Inter Cert after all, but had done very well. My mother was very impressed that they would take the time to call to our house to tell me this, but I didn't share her feeling of gratitude. I was very unresponsive, almost bordering on being rude to both of them. I did not have a good thing to say about anyone who was part of the Church back then, not after my experiences in Bessborough House. In hindsight I think the head sister was trying to let me know that I had the ability to return to education but I didn't have the confidence in myself to hear that. The last year had really knocked me back. I couldn't wait for them to leave. 'Nosy biddies,' I thought. And when the opportunity was offered again by the people I worked for, it was too late. It just wasn't meant for me. As it turned out, I would return to education, but not for many years.

When my son's first birthday had come around I was distraught. I had managed to keep it together for a year, often operating on autopilot, but I couldn't maintain the facade when his first birthday came up. Who did he look like? How much had he grown? Was he happy where he was? The desire to find a way to get him back came flooding in. My solution was to go out and get as drunk as I possibly could, drunk enough to be oblivious to the pain. This is something I did for the first three or four years after his birth. The last time this happened was early in my marriage. That night I drank almost a full bottle of vodka but couldn't get drunk. This frightened me so much that I stopped drinking altogether for a time. I would have to find another way to handle this. The need to take the edge off, even if it was not a constant one, could have become very dangerous. Sometimes I would ruminate over the whole thing, wondering if I had done the right thing, second-guessing myself about whether I should have insisted on looking for him when my boyfriend proposed to me, if I should have made it a condition of getting married. But that old voice that told me you couldn't expect someone else to pay for your mistakes insisted otherwise. It had never been on the table, from him or from me. Wasn't I lucky that he would want me when I had one child, never mind taking on two of them? There was that feeling of worthlessness, that internal message of not being wanted just for myself. Then I would wonder if I should just tell everyone and go and look for my son. Then the twisted thinking loop would move around to whether it would be right to look for him at all. If he was happy in his new home, if he had everything I couldn't give him, did I have the right to smash into that perfect life and disrupt it? In my head he had the ideal life, the life that, as it would turn out, my other children would not have. Round and round my thoughts would go like an express train to nowhere because I couldn't ever see a way to do anything about all of this.

The only thing that kept me going at times was the knowledge that my son was in a stable home. He had two parents who weren't scrabbling around for money. He would have a good education, a good family life and opportunities to make something of himself. I often wondered what it would be like if he looked for me when he was older. This brought up such feelings of dread that I usually tried to push that thought away. What if he hated me? What if he blamed me? I couldn't bear the thought of the judgement so I kept on pushing everything down. I got married in 1977 and our first son was born in 1978. I thought of my son in England. He would be four years of age now. Could I look for him? Get him back? But with each year it almost became easier to live with the realisation that I would never see him again. It became easier to push everything down even further. But something that huge can never be totally pushed down, and when I least expected I would remember the feel of him in my body, the weight of him in my arms. I would remember the days spent in London, days waiting for his arrival. I would remember the week in Guy's Hospital and the day I handed him over to his new family and the grief would wash over me in waves. I would long to see him and curse the decision I made not to have photos sent to me. I would decide that I was going to look for him, I was going to contact the agency that I had worked with, but in the cold light of day I would chicken out. Over the years I had hidden my secret so well that I began to forget some of the details. I never forgot about my son, but I couldn't remember the name of the agency or the support worker I had spent so much time with. It was as if my mind decided to delete some of the details of that time. If it arose I pushed it back down and concentrated on the family I had now. But in later years I began to let go of the secret little by little. I told my sister and some close friends and they didn't judge me.

It was like releasing the steam from a pressure cooker, but really slowly. I never told his father or his sister and as time went on it seemed impossible that I could ever break that silence. Not until that day in August 2017 when so much water had passed under that particular bridge that I'm still not sure to this day what inspired me to break the silence.

13

Breaking the Silence

'Breaking our silence means living in existential courage.'
– Mary Daly, *Gyn/Ecology*

August 2017

As I walked towards the town I wondered what reason he had given for meeting me. When I had asked him if we could meet to discuss something he had agreed immediately. He didn't even ask me what I wanted to discuss. He knew I was writing about my time in Bessborough House, so maybe he thought I wanted to talk about that. He had promised not to say anything to the others until we had spoken, a promise I found out later that he hadn't kept. Maybe he wouldn't even turn up. If he had any inkling of what he was about to hear maybe he would have run for the hills. I had been grappling with the idea of telling him, of telling my family about my second baby, for years. In the early days after the adoption I was so traumatised that the only way to cope was to push down everything that had happened, down so deep that years could go by without any adverse effects. As time went by I wondered if my son would arrive at my door one day, asking if I was his mother. How would I explain him to everyone? Because I knew that if he did appear on my doorstep I would never hide him away. I had no reason to doubt that his adoptive parents would have told him about me, as I had asked them to on that day so many years ago, so it was feasible that he could turn up or try to search for me. At other times, as the years went by, I wondered why he wasn't searching for me. There was so much in the media about the mother and baby homes, so much about adoptees searching for their birth mothers, that I was half-expecting a phone call one day. I had never planned on searching for him, I didn't think that would be the right thing to do. I had spent so much time when I was waiting for him to be born trying to choose the best parents for him, making sure he went to a family that could offer him everything I couldn't. I had given up my right to interfere in his life and I always felt strongly that the search should be initiated by him. If he was happy enough where he was I didn't have the right to crash into his life.

When I thought of telling the various people involved I would try to imagine their reactions. Would they be angry, disappointed in me, never speak to me again? Would the telling of this secret create a huge rift in my family, one that would never be healed? I always imagined the worst when I thought of it and by the time I had gone through all the scenarios in my head I would just give up, push it all down and tell myself that it was better to get on with my life and not say anything. However, over the last few years the urge to talk about him had become so insistent that the words often threatened to just spill from my throat and it was a miracle that I didn't shout it from the rooftops at times. Now that there were such open conversations about mother and baby homes I could talk about that part of my life more freely. My eldest granddaughter had asked me about it. What was it like to be in one of the homes, what had happened there, how had I felt? It was good to talk to her about this but it always felt like half the story was choked off. Only a few people knew about the other child who had the same father but was never spoken about. I had spent years going over every reason why it would be better to say nothing, to bring this secret to the grave with me, but I knew that even as I was still having this internal debate with myself, today was the day that I would tell him about his son, the son who had been born in Guy's Hospital, London, in 1974, the son he didn't know about. Then I would have to tell my daughter, the daughter that I had brought home from Bessborough House all those years ago, that she had a brother she had never known about. I felt sick at the thought of what I was about to do, but I knew there was no stopping this now.

One evening last year when her father had been over visiting the two of them arrived at my door unexpectedly. Why did they decide to pay me an impromptu visit that night? And what had stopped me from telling them there and then? It was unusual to get a visit from both of them. It was inevitable that we would bump into each other from time to time as he always came to Ireland to celebrate birthdays, or his grandchildren's special days, such as christenings, birthdays, communions or confirmations. But these occasions were always planned. His daughter loved him and they spent a lot of time together whenever he visited Athlone, but visits to my house were not usually on the agenda when he was home. They must have registered the surprise on my face when I answered the door that evening.

'We were out for a drive and thought we'd call to visit you,' my daughter said.

I invited them in. He had brought a bottle of wine with him and I rooted out some cheese and crackers. We sat around the coffee table in the sitting room chatting about everything and anything, everything trivial and nothing that should have been spoken about. We covered the price of housing in Ireland, the pros and cons of medication for cholesterol; anything but personal issues, anything but what was foremost in my mind that night. 'What has brought them here?' I thought again. 'Was this the night I was supposed to tell them?' I could tell them both together. Maybe that would be easier than telling them separately. I had always thought that if I was going to do this I would tell him first. After all, he had a right to know that he had a son. Then I would tell my daughter, even though I would find that harder than telling him. If I was supposed to tell them that night the opportunity was lost. When it came to the push, even though the words were ready to be spoken they seemed to be lodged in my throat. It's hard to explain why such a secret is so difficult to let go of. It was so huge and lodged so deep that it seemed impossible to move it even though it was trying desperately to get to the surface. Once it emerged into the light of day there would be no going back. As they left I decided that I had driven myself mad enough with all of this and I was going to put it to one side for now.

But this year another opportunity had presented itself. My granddaughter wanted me to go out with them for her birthday. Although there was nothing else I wanted to do more than celebrate her birthday with her, I felt uncomfortable with the idea of all us going out together. It was out of the norm. But my granddaughter wanted both her grandparents with her for this birthday. I came up with several reasons why I couldn't attend. I had a prior engagement. I had to work until 7.00 p.m. Maybe her mother would prefer if they went out with her granddad without me being there? But my granddaughter was insistent and she countered every one of my arguments.

'It's my birthday and I'm inviting you.'

'It will be my treat.'

'It's important to me that everyone is together.'

In the end resistance was futile and I had gone along. When I arrived at my daughter's house that evening I greeted her father with a hug. I always did this when we met but now it felt different, because now I was thinking of how he would react when I told him about his son. We got a taxi to the restaurant and everyone seemed to be in good form. During the evening we found ourselves alone at the table. I'm not sure where everyone else had disappeared to, maybe to have a smoke or to use the toilets. I leaned across the table and asked him if he would meet me during the week as I had something I wanted to talk to him about. I couldn't believe I was actually doing this. It was as if I was watching someone else leaning over the table and asking him. I asked him not to mention it to anyone else until we had spoken. This was it; I had made the first step. I felt sick with nerves. I told myself that I didn't have to go through with it. I could change my mind, make up some excuse for meeting him, or even cancel the meeting. Now, as I neared the hotel where we had arranged to meet, I could feel my stomach churning with nerves.

The lighting was dim inside the bar of the hotel. I had arrived before him and I bought a coffee while I waited. I had hoped he would be here before me. The waiting would only increase my anxiety. I wished I could have something stronger, but I needed to keep a clear head. I sat near the front entrance so that I wouldn't miss him coming in. I was keyed up. I couldn't relax. When he spotted me he came over to say hello and asked if I wanted anything. I said I was fine and he went to get a coffee for himself. When he came back he sat at the opposite end of the table. We made small talk for a few minutes, then he asked me what it was I wanted to talk about. I could feel the words rushing up to my mouth, wanting to spill out. I had thought of nothing else since the night of the meal except telling my daughter and her father that there was another baby, born in 1974, a son he didn't know anything about and a brother she had never been aware of. Now I thought of all the fears I had about what might happen once I said the words. The ingrained fear of anyone finding out, a throwback from those days in the 1970s, was overwhelming, especially in the days leading up to the meeting. 'You don't need to do this, you can tell him it's about the book,' I thought, which would make sense, as they all knew I had been talking about writing about my experiences in Bessborough House. I felt sick at the thought of what I was about to do and what would happen after today. I knew that my daughter had the right to know but I also knew that she would be angry, angry and hurt, and that it would probably take a long time for her to forgive me, if she ever did. The rest of my children would never look at me in the same way. And what about my grandchildren? I was very close to my eldest granddaughter. What would she think of me when she heard this? Was there any point in going ahead? Would it be better to let sleeping dogs lie? What they didn't know wouldn't hurt them. I was standing on a cliff edge, about to step off. Was I mad? How was I even going to start this conversation? Should I have told her first? Should I have asked the two of them to meet me? What was the right thing to do? But there was no right or wrong way to approach this. Anyone who saw me walking along that day or sitting at this table would not have guessed at the tsunami of thoughts and feelings rising up beneath the surface. All they would have seen was a middle-aged woman, maybe deep in thought, perhaps on her way to meet someone for a coffee, or going to town to do some shopping. Do we ever really know what anyone is going through when we pass each other in the street, and smile or nod or give a greeting? Imagining the reactions of everyone involved that day was one thing, but the real-life reactions after the telling would turn out to be quite another thing.

All of these thoughts flew through my head in the minute or two it took me to answer him. I wanted to be discreet, I didn't want anyone sitting near us to overhear what I was about to say, so I asked him if he would sit nearer to me. He didn't move. 'I'm grand here,' he said. I asked him again to move nearer so no one would hear what I said, but he made no effort to do so. 'Okay,' I thought, 'here goes.' 'I want to tell you something and I need to say it in one go so don't stop me until I'm finished,' I said. I thought I would struggle with trying to explain everything that had happened and how I dealt with it, but once I started it was as if I couldn't stop. It poured out from me. 'Do you remember just after we brought our little girl home from Bessborough House, I told you that I might be pregnant again?' I'm not sure if he remembered this, and to be honest I probably didn't give him much of a chance to respond to me. Like a runaway train the story flew out of the 44-year-old tunnel of suppression. 'Do you remember that I told you a few days later that I had made a mistake? I knew then that I was pregnant but I didn't want to get married. I didn't know how to tell you. I couldn't face the thought of getting married. I'm sorry, but I didn't feel the same about you, about us. I was sixteen. All I could see was my life gone down an irrevocable trap of marriage and children. I asked someone who knew my father if they would make contact with him and see if I could go over to him. I needed to get out of Athlone. I couldn't ask my mother for his address. I couldn't let her know I was pregnant. This person offered to make contact with my father and when they did he wrote to me and asked me if I would like to come over and work with him for a few months. I had not told anyone else that I was pregnant. I hadn't gone to a doctor. I was too scared of anyone finding out. The night before I went over to England my grand-mother called to our house and confronted me about being pregnant again. She made me tell my mother. I can't remember whether I broke off our relationship before or after I had made the arrangement to go to England. I spent a couple of weeks with my father and his partner but it wasn't working out so I went to stay with someone else until my baby was born. He was born in Guy's Hospital and the labour was very difficult but he was beautiful. I spent a week with him and then I handed him over myself to his adoptive parents. You have a son and I'm sorry that I have never told you this before, but I couldn't see any other way out back then, and over the years any time I thought I might say something there would be some crisis in the family and I thought that at least he was okay, he was away from all the madness, he was safe.'

I don't think I took a breath while I told him. It was as if once I started I couldn't stop until I got it all out, until there was nothing left to say. I looked up at him nervously. I didn't know how he was going to react to all of this. I was expecting shock, disbelief, hurt, anger, anything but what I saw. It was so unexpected, well apart from the inevitable, 'And he's mine?'

Why is that always the question asked? Why would I be telling him all this if he was not his son? 'Yes, he is your son.'

When I looked over at him, he was smiling and he said, 'I have a son.' His response threw me. I had been ready for the anger, the blaming, the judgement. I had my defence prepared. But now I was the one thrown on the back foot as he seemed to be okay with what I had told him. He already had an adult son and his comment made no sense to me. He was actually smiling. For now, anyway. I told him I was sorry, I didn't know why I was telling him now, but the need to do so was so strong that I couldn't hold it in any longer. Our daughter didn't know yet and I told him how nervous I was about telling her, how hard it was going to be. He said that he would help me, we would tell her together. I was physically shaking all over. I think I was in more shock than he was. But then again, I didn't really know this man so it was presumptuous of me to judge his level of shock. We had an intense relationship for maybe two or two-and-a-half years when I was between the ages of fourteen and sixteen. Any interaction after that was time spent with our daughter and grandchildren or the occasional visits to our flat after I had been married. I really didn't know this man, and this would become clearer as the days went on, as his reaction changed totally.

In spite of all the scenarios I imagined when I told them, I don't believe I was truly prepared for the repercussions of breaking my silence that day and for how far the fallout of this revelation would spread. I didn't know whether I wanted to sit or stand, walk away or run away. I asked him if there was anything he wanted to ask me. I knew I had spilled everything out in a rush and I felt I owed him the time to go over everything. I also thought that once we had told our daughter that evening I would not have to see him again and that any explanations or clarification he needed would be done with today. I didn't realise how much blame and shame I still carried, how responsible I felt for everything that had happened to me in the 1970s, including getting pregnant. I was still operating from a place of defence, even though there was no need to. He surprised me more when he got up from his seat and came over to hug me, saying he was sorry that I had to go through all of this on my own. I didn't know how to respond. I couldn't really reciprocate the hug, but I did thank him for saying that and I apologised again for not telling him. I felt bad and I couldn't figure out why. There had been two of us in it and while I could take full responsibility for keeping the knowledge of his son from him, I didn't know why I still felt that everything that had happened had been my fault. He went to get me another coffee and I sat back trying to figure out what was going on. When he came back he asked me questions about that time. He said that he knew I had gone to London, and as he was there too around that time and had often looked out to see if he could spot me. He was adamant that if I had told him he would have taken care of the child. I was honest and told him that I knew he would have married me but the only real concrete decision I could stand by was that I was not going to get married. We had been so close to doing so, even going as far as attending marriage preparation classes, but I knew even back then that I was too young. I told him again that I was sorry that I had kept this from him, but I always felt that our son was better off where he was. There had been a lot of chaos in our family and my own marriage had fallen apart. I really believed that our son was the lucky one, he had escaped all the upheaval of the various family dramas, and that was something I had never deviated from. My defence was my age and the lifestyle we lived at the time. It was all fun back then to go out drinking or get stoned, but that was the life for young people, which we both were, not the basis for rearing a family. My feelings had changed totally after our daughter was born and I didn't see marriage for the sake of a child or a pregnancy as an option. Again, I felt I had to have a defence as if I had been at fault in some way. At some stage my granddaughter arrived at the hotel. I was relieved as it meant we could take a break from talking about this for a while. We had decided to tell our daughter together in my house that evening, so I left shortly after my granddaughter arrived and went home to prepare for the coming evening. I was nervous. I sensed the first rumblings of the earthquake, but I was resolute in my decision to keep going. As I made my way home, I knew that the coming evening would not be easy.

I spent the rest of the day trying to keep busy but I couldn't settle down. By the time he arrived I was a nervous wreck. He had brought a bottle of wine but much as I would have liked a glass, I wanted to keep a clear head. We discussed how we would break the news to her. He suggested putting her between us on the couch as we told her. 'She's a grown woman! Are you mad?' I thought, but I kept it to myself, which was difficult, as I was so keyed up. I tried to keep calm and suggested that it might be better if she decided where to sit. As we waited I could hardly hear anything he said, I just wanted my daughter to arrive. When I opened the door to her I felt that she sensed something was up. There is no easy way to tell someone the news I had to tell her. It was one of the hardest things I have had to do in my life and I could see how shocked she was. I had hoped that she would stay and we could talk about it but she left as soon as she could. I think she couldn't sit and listen to any more. He thought it had gone very well and I wondered if he really knew her at all. I knew that there was a long and difficult road ahead for all of us, and it was going to take a lot of time to process and work through this news. No, this hadn't gone well at all, but I had to trust that it was the right thing to do, that in time it would bring some sort of healing to all of us.

I could go through the list of who supported me and who didn't in the coming days as I began to let the rest of my family and some friends know about my son. Who listened and who didn't, who used the situation to get all the details and then talk about it, who was genuinely concerned and who wanted salacious gossip. But what good would that do? People react to things in different ways and my main concern was the reaction of my children. This was traumatic for them. I had known about my son for over 40 years, they were only finding out now, and I can only speak of this from my experience. It was as if an earthquake had hit our family, with the hidden energy of guilt, shame and secrecy brushing against the energy of truth and transparency, resulting in a seismic shift that moved all the parameters of our family relationships. This shift would result in the destruction of all we had known but it also had the potential to create relationships based on newer and more authentic understandings. Only time would tell. Even now I can see that my perspective was skewed by my deep-seated feelings of shame and guilt. The need to keep things quiet, to hide what had happened from the neighbours and, above all, never to air your dirty linen in public, had driven my decisions so far. This would change today. This thinking, which was a throwback from the past, had not stopped me from bringing my daughter home from Bessborough or on insisting that she knew who she was and knew who her parents were, but the shame of the second pregnancy had been too much to stand up to. What had been ingrained in me from the time of my birth, the message of original sin, the idea that we constantly needed to confess and be cleansed, along with my experiences in the 1970s, coloured my perspective on what was happening, so that I was in constant defensive mode. I was like a warrior going into battle all the time and it was exhausting. I wanted to be open to how others were, to how this news was affecting them, but I was also on guard all the time, finding ways to justify and vindicate myself. This didn't make it easy for anyone in the early days after I broke my silence.

The day after telling my daughter I had arranged to meet my granddaughter. I really wanted to see her alone, to explain what had happened so many years ago, but her grandfather came with her and his response to what I had told him was very different from the previous day. He insisted he would have reared this child, and if he couldn't one of his sisters would have taken him in. He seemed judgemental and angry and his response was very different from the hug and 'I have a son' comment of the previous day. I was exhausted. I felt cornered, judged and found guilty all over again. I had thought I had done all the explaining I needed to do. I had told him what he needed to know and I did not intend to interfere in any search he made for our son. All I asked was that he be careful, take it slowly and take what our son might be feeling into account. I myself did not intend to begin a search at the moment. That was something I would have to give a lot of thought to, but I would never stand in his way. I felt judged for that as well. Judged for being pregnant, for being pregnant a second time, for not telling anyone, for not starting a search. Again, it was the woman who was deemed to be in the wrong. I can remember thinking, 'I knew I would get all the blame.' The months that followed were very difficult. I was physically sick for the whole of that first week and found it difficult to focus on work, or anything else for that matter. I had begun the process of telling the rest of my immediate family and then some close friends who hadn't known. I would not have gotten through that time without the support of my friends, who were always ready to listen to me and who didn't judge. As my family became more used to the news their different reactions caused rifts, shakes and re-assembling of relationships. The aftershocks would reverberate for some time.

The greatest tragedy of all of this was that after his father had instigated a search for him we found out that our son had died some years earlier. This was something I had never imagined hearing. My fear when the search began was that my son would blame me or that he would find it difficult to understand why it was his father and not I who had searched for him. I never imagined all of this would end with another loss. Even though I wasn't sure about searching for my son I had made contact with

Barnardo's Post-Adoption Service. They were the only agency in the country running a support group for birth mothers and they provided a safe space where I could discuss what was happening and explore the options open to me. Finding out about my son's death was a huge blow, one that I am still coming to terms with, and the birth mothers' group again proved to be an invaluable source of support during this time. I had four children from my marriage and our eldest son had died in 2002, so I was all too aware of the impact of such a loss on a mother. Finding out that my son in England had died was devastating, but I couldn't help but think of the pain his mother was going through. She was the one who had undertaken to love him and care for him, the one who had watched him grow from baby to young boy and then to young man. My experience told me that she too would have struggled for years to make sense of such a loss. I decided that I was not going to go any further in a search for information about him. I had one week with him, this woman had reared him and had been there for him throughout his growing years. I had my memories, and I felt that she and his family in England should be left with theirs.

I got married only three years after I had been in England, three years after I had given my son up for adoption. The need to have a normal life and not be 'one of those girls', was the driving force behind many of my decisions back then. The need to run as far away as possible from my experiences of Bessborough House and London, to be 'good', to be someone other people wanted me to be, to be wanted, kept me from knowing who I really was for a long time. It would take me years to realise there is no such thing as 'girls like you'. In my attempts to live this hypothetical normal life I was in fact living the life recommended by my mother and grandmother. I was living the life espoused by the Church and State in twentieth-century Ireland. I was building a family unit that was kept safe at the cost of both of my eldest children. I was turning my back on a part of myself. It is almost impossible to explain this to someone who hasn't gone through this experience. What they may see is the abandonment, not the ethos that drove it, an ethos of shame, secrecy and outward 'good living'. Breaking the silence was like trying to move a gigantic boulder that was deeply embedded in the earth around it, so deeply embedded that you fear that its removal will cause an upheaval of the earth akin to an earthquake. What else will be damaged when you move this boulder? How far will the earth move and shift when you do this? What will replace the void left after letting the secret go? I am still figuring out some of the answers to these questions. I am still learning to have compassion for myself, to be less defensive and to have compassion for those who have been hurt by this revelation. My story is mine alone, but it also impacts those around me. Regardless of their different reactions, each person involved in this story is important, each person has the right to respond in their way. If I had to put one word on how I feel after bringing the past into the light, it would be 'freedom', but it is a freedom tinged with sorrow, with loss. It's like a part of me had been holding its breath for over 40 years. Now I can breathe.

14

Some Final Thoughts

'Between you and your mother there was only a membrane, wafer thin.'

– Edna O'Brien, *A Pagan Place*

Writing this memoir has been like taking a journey. What began as a desire to tell my story slowly turned into something more complex and nuanced as the memoir began to take shape. Reflecting back on the process I can see how my perspective on my past, and what I had experienced, changed as a result of putting pen to paper. My viewpoint has broadened. Perhaps this is something to do with my age and life experience. Perhaps it is something that happens when we are willing to take the time to scrutinise our memories. When we do this, we can approach them in a more thoughtful and less reactive manner. When writing about painful memories, there is sometimes a tendency to want to get them down on paper as quickly as possible, to just get on with telling the story. After all, I was there for all of it, so it shouldn't be so difficult, should it? But it was difficult, and the process was not made any easier by the publication of the Mother and Baby Homes Commission of Investigation Final Report in October 2020. The report, which was made public while I was in the process of finishing the memoir, was difficult to read. At times I found myself overwhelmed with sadness while reading the accounts of others' suffering and their struggles in coming to terms with their experiences in the mother and baby homes. There were times when I was consumed with anger when reading of people hidebound by bureaucracy in their search for their birth families. Some of the accounts from former staff of Bessborough House, of which I had first-hand knowledge, were also very unsettling. Seeing, in an official document, a statement declaring that the girls and women who resided in Bessborough House were happy to have their given name taken from them and use a false name, when I knew this was not the case, nearly sent me over the edge. Statements about how these girls, abandoned by their families and taken in by the nuns, were provided with solace in their time of need, were galling to read. As were the statements about how the nuns in question attempted to bolster the confidence and self-esteem of the young girls and women in their care. Suggesting that young girls, especially those who were minors, as I was, were morally corrupt or somehow fully culpable for their condition does not strike me as a method of building up self-esteem or confidence. It never dawned on me when I was at Bessborough House to question why those who had a duty of care towards us were instead sanctioning the hiding away of girls who were pregnant without questioning what had happened to them. It never dawned on me to question why the State would pay to have a woman or young girl kept in Bessborough House, while the Church ensured that the responsibility for what had happened to her fell on her, and her alone. There is something very warped about some of the statements that are being accepted today, in 2021, regarding the behaviour of some of the staff in the mother and baby homes. There were times when I had to down tools and walk away from work, leave my house and get outside to create some space between the emotions I was experiencing and what I was writing about. There is no doubt that this is a subject fraught with emotional minefields. My intention was not to write a memoir that was driven by negative emotion, but rather to write my own truth. What I have written is what happened as I remember it and as I experienced it. It is my story. It does not reflect the experience of any other woman, but there is one common thread that runs through all our stories, the thread of shame.

Writing our story brings meaning to our lives. The Greek philosopher Aristotle (382–322 BC) was one of the first to propose this idea. He also suggested that in writing our memories, the actions of our lives, we not only bring meaning to our own lives, but we also make our histories shareable. Perhaps the writing of my memoir will resonate with others and they will recognise something of their own life in it. I do not know. But I do know that when asked back in 2011 why I wanted to write about this I could not come up with a valid answer straight away. I wanted to tell my story, but I couldn't articulate the reason why I wanted to do so. All I knew was that there was something deep inside me that wanted to put words on the experience, to speak of what had happened in Bessborough House, to bring it out into the light. Maybe it was because as a mature student in All Hallows College, Drumcondra, I was finally beginning to speak, though hesitantly, about my past, something I had done only with close family and friends before this. Maybe it was because I was in the company of a number of religious figures, lecturers who were priests and nuns, who seemed humane and compassionate. Perhaps I wanted to gain some understanding of how all of this had happened in Ireland, in a past that didn't seem so long ago to me. Maybe I just wanted to make sense of it all. For whatever reason, it was there that I first began to toy with the idea of writing. In the back of my mind there was always the thought of my son in England, the son that most of my family did not yet know about. How could I write about Bessborough House and not write about him, and how could I write about him if I hadn't told anyone about him? So the idea of writing would be taken out and examined, and then shelved, in a process very similar to the one I went through when I thought about telling my family of his existence.

Over the years the desire to write and the fear of what this would entail instilled a deep sense of conflict within me. At times I would begin the process, even sharing some of the work. The open mic nights in All Hallows provided a safe venue to do this. But it was not until 2017, when I was again back in education completing a Masters in Maynooth University, that I finally divulged my secret and could begin to write the story in a coherent manner. Not straight away, mind you, as the aftermath from the revelation took a number of years to settle. It was 2020 before I began the serious process of writing. The build-up to the writing, the time it took before I could even think of commencing, was similar to the build-up to telling my family about my son. I began to recognise the triggers that reinforce the habit of silence, the throwbacks from the past that make it so difficult for women to speak out. Even now, with all that is in the public domain, it still remains difficult for women to speak about their personal experiences, to take their past out and have it openly scrutinised. Even after the publication of the report, patience is needed in allowing women to come forward and talk. A culture of silence has committed them to a prison of 'not telling', and while more and more voices are welcomed there are still those who live back in the era of 'not letting the neighbours know', or in some cases even their own husbands and family. I don't think people today realise the extent of 'the stench of shame' that followed unmarried mothers in twentieth-century Ireland, a concept the psychologist Maureen Gaffney refers to in an article published in the *Irish Times*, which examines how shame and guilt, which were foisted on women in the name of religion, have a long-term effect. In her article 'The Land of Mother and Baby Homes', published on 16 January 2021, she offers an understanding of just how deep the shame of being an unmarried mother goes, and how far it follows the women who were incarcerated there.

I had my own questions also, questions I did not realise I had, questions that only began to emerge in the writing of this memoir. Others have theirs. My initial response to the question of why I wanted to write this was in order to tell my story, to understand why everything had happened as it had. But it was only as I wrote that I began to notice that I had a tendency to fall into self-explanation, a need to constantly explain my thoughts and actions, to justify my behaviour. It was almost as if I was on trial, and I was my own judge and jury. For instance, when I write about being in a sexual relationship at such a young age, I say that 'I was not using any protection', instead of 'we were not using any protection'. There were, after all, two of us in this relationship. When I realised this tendency to self-blame I began to ask myself why I was doing this. Was I such a bad person? Had I done something terrible? Writing helped me see just how deep the 'stench of shame' had penetrated, and how far it had followed me. Almost 50 years later and here I was, still feeling somehow responsible for everything that had happened back then. While I knew in my mind that this was not true, it still shocked me to realise how deeply that shame had infiltrated my whole psyche, even to this day. At times I found myself writing whole paragraphs in an almost apologetic manner, paragraphs that I deleted in anger as I began to realise the extent of the damage that was done by the constant instilling of shame and guilt in the past. The words 'there are girls like you' loomed large at times. I was also aware of the constant see-sawing between wanting to blame others and then feeling a deep need to protect them. The constant need to protect the ones in charge to make sure people are not portrayed in a bad light can be viewed as a noble objective. It is also a direct result of gaslighting, a phenomenon that occurs when those who are in a position of power, when those who are responsible for our care, manipulate us instead into thinking that it is all our fault, that we are the ones to blame. This realisation caused me to look again at my story.

Where did this feeling of guilt and shame come from? And why was it still affecting me so long after the events of the 1970s? The Catholic Church were experts in making us feel guilty, but they also did a good job of making us feel ashamed, a feeling that causes far more damage. Maureen Gaffney remarks that shame 'is a more primitive feeling, a feeling of being exposed, stripped naked, degraded'. It evokes the most primal of human fears, the fear of being cast out of our community. It was through the use of language, not brute force, that young women and girls were broken. In mother and baby homes the nuns did not need to use physical violence to crush the spirit of the women. Instead, labels such as 'fallen women', 'first and second offenders', 'sinners', 'morally weak' and 'corrupt' were used to separate women from other women, from society, from their families and communities. The cost to me of this toxic mixture of guilt and shame has been a tendency always to second-guess myself, to veer between indecision and impulsiveness, to take more responsibility than I need to, to be overly self-critical. For others it has resulted in all-consuming depression, anxiety and panic attacks. My hope is that anyone reading this memoir who has been in a similar situation will learn to be forgiving towards themselves, that they will recognise that it was those who blamed us who were in fact culpable. Those who should have provided care and support instead turned out to be our tormentors. This self-critical element, which crept into my writing unconsciously, helped me to see just how programmed I had become. It also led me to another process in the writing, that of scrutinising which elements of my history are my story and which belong to another story, one that is not mine at all.

Whose story is this anyway? If it is mine, as I clearly knew it was, then why was there so much shame and guilt still floating around in it, still coming through in the writing? Why did I still feel so trapped in my past? I began to examine how my story, my personal experience, could still evoke these powerful feelings that I thought I had left behind. When I went back and looked at the details I began to see that my story was not mine alone. It was also a story that had become entangled with another very powerful one, the story of 'girls like you'. At times it was hard to see where my story and this other one began and ended. I began to see how my story and the story that had been constructed as far back as the setting up of the Free State, and even earlier, had collided, becoming inexorably enmeshed, almost inseparable. At that time, the then Taoiseach Éamon de Valera, who would go on to become president of Ireland, had a vision of a nation full of people who preferred frugality to comfort, spiritual advancement to modernisation. This was the root of the message repeated again and again in mother and baby homes in Ireland. It was better to suffer for your sins; no pain relief for you. In a speech given in 1943 de Valera referred to this new State as being made up of 'fields and villages joyous with the sounds of industry, with romping sturdy children, the contests of athletic youths and the laughter of happy maidens'. In *Moral Monopoly: The Rise and Fall of the Catholic Church in Modern Ireland* (1998) Tom Inglis provides an interesting insight into how these ideas formed a nation that could be controlled by the Church as well as the State. As long as the romping sturdy children came from a legitimate married couple then everything was fine. For those who didn't comply with this vision, life was very different. I began to realise that my story was not simply my story but one that had become entangled with a fantasy story, a story where motherhood was restricted to the married woman, a story where the single woman who dared to attempt to keep her child, to be a mother to her child, was in danger of being ousted from her community and her family. There was little mention of the men, who were complicit in the pregnancies, sometimes through rape and incest. Women bore the brunt of the social and, at times, legal discrimination. It is really important when reflecting on our story that we realise where our story begins and ends and where this national rhetoric butts in. We must be careful to own only our own history, not that which has been forced on us. The story of 'girls like you' is a fabrication, there is no such thing as the good woman or the bad woman; there are women. There is no such thing as the deserving mother and the undeserving mother; there are mothers.

Of all the things that saddened me the most when writing this memoir, it was the realisation that a whole generation of women had been sold a lie about motherhood. This lie was used to give power to the women who obeyed the rules of society and to take power away from others by using innocent children as pawns in a power game. In order to have any power, any voice in the home or community, the Irish mother had to be morally incorrupt, above reproach, virtuous and chaste. That meant unquestioning loyalty to the Church, often even before their own families. While this was not the case in every household, it was sufficiently prevalent to ensure that the mother and baby homes were full for a number of years. Motherhood – that mystical, opaque and mercurial idea – which in Ireland is based on the myth of a woman who can give birth without having sex, was the goal imposed on women. This notion encouraged women to turn away from their own daughters if they did not live up to this impossible standard. It encouraged mothers to turn their backs on the 'becoming' mother who was not married. It separated mothers into categories of good and bad, worthy and unworthy. I am very conscious that the issue of mothering is not restricted to the biological birth process, that there are many ways of mothering, but the issue I am concerned with here is the routine practice of tearing babies away from their biological mothers, a practice that was carried on wholesale in twentieth-century Ireland, under the auspices of Church and State. It could only have been carried out by elevating the power of the Church above the power of the mother. This is evident when we think of the number of married women who could not attend their children's baptisms and even, at times, funerals, if they had not been churched in accordance with Catholic Church teaching.

The practice of separating children from their 'unworthy' mothers was facilitated by an unfailing adherence to the story introduced by the State and Church of twentieth-century Ireland, a story that was specifically aimed at the women who were becoming mothers outside of marriage. I call this a story because that is exactly what it was, a made-up story, designed to control not only the lives of women but of all Irish society. It was tied in with the unhealthy obsession with sex and sexuality that the Church perpetuated. While a lot has been written about this unhealthy interest in the sexual behaviour of its flock, we have only to think of Archbishop of Dublin John Charles McQuaid's abhorrence of the mention of all things to do with the female body or reproduction, or his single-handed campaign to ban the use of tampons in Ireland, to see how far this went. This is documented in historian Diarmaid Ferriter's book *Occasions of Sin: Sex and Society in Modern Ireland* (2009). One of the primary victims of this story was the legitimate birth mother, who was relegated to a position outside of the national narrative if she was unmarried. In this story there is room for the reverend mother, the mother superior, the mother general and the mother Church, the good mother who will take in the baby born out of marriage. But there is no room for the mother who is carrying the child, but is not married, who does not uphold the moral teaching of a dictatorial Church and State. This is a story that kept a whole society enthralled, paving the way for a mass rejection of women by their own mothers, by their own families, a rejection that was encouraged and sanctioned by the State and Church. It didn't even matter whether the women had been defiant or defiled, they were deemed to be sinners either way. Is it any wonder that sifting out our own story is so difficult? Is it any wonder that we are filled with shame and guilt? Is it any wonder that a whole generation of women grew up without knowing what it was to be a mother?

The collision of the national story and women's personal individual histories resulted in a generation of young women and girls being incarcerated. Their children were forcibly removed from them, at times growing up without the knowledge of where they come from. Swiss psychologist Carl Jung posits that without our myth, without our story, we are unrooted. The policies of Church and State, which kept such rigid control of a whole nation, through fear, shame and excess guilt, have resulted in generations who are without roots. We need to tell our story; it is no longer a matter of wanting to tell it or wanting to make sense of it. It is imperative that voices are heard and that in the hearing we untangle ourselves from the lie that was told for so long in Ireland.

This question of why a mother would turn against her own daughter was one that dogged me throughout the writing of the memoir. Why would mothers in Ireland do this en masse? The previous lines have addressed this but something that I kept returning to during the writing was the ancient Greek myth of Demeter and Persephone, a story that was told to explain how the seasons of the year came to be. Demeter was the goddess of the earth. When her daughter Persephone was abducted by the god of Hades Demeter heard her daughter's cry from under the earth, even though she was not near her at the time. She went to Zeus, king of all the gods, and told him that until her daughter was found she would refuse to produce any more crops. There would be no harvest and the very food that kept men alive would be withheld until her daughter returned to the surface of the earth. An agreement was reached whereby Persephone would spend part of the year underground in Hades and part of it above ground with her mother. It was only in the seasons when Persephone was allowed to come back to the surface that Demeter produced any crops. Without the mother–daughter relationship the world becomes sterile; all of society suffers, not just women. In ancient cultures the mother–daughter relationship was deified. It was considered divine. Where has that divinity disappeared to? Where was the God of the Church when women were incarcerated in mother and baby homes in Ireland? Who heard their cries from under the earth? And who will account now for the unrooted children, the devastated mothers, the lost years? Will a mother superior raise her voice to admit her cruelty, to take responsibility? Or are those pseudo mothers just as much victims of a rotten regime as the young women and childless couples have been? A whole generation of Irish women was handed down a model of motherhood based on blind obedience to a Church that turned its back on them when they most needed its support. It was a model based on obedience, virtue and chastity, not natural love and connection. The idea that there were only two types of mother in Irish society, the good mother or the unworthy one, resulted in the opportunity for mothering being stolen from several generations of women.

During the writing of this memoir, I have often turned my thoughts to Demeter, whose connection to her daughter allowed her to hear Persephone's cries, even from beneath the ground. I have had to search for a way to find compassion for myself, for the young fifteen- and sixteen-year-old girl I was, for my mother, who was a victim of Church teaching, for the mother I became until I knew better. I have had to find compassion for the adult woman who held on to a secret – some would say for too long – but writing this memoir has helped me understand why I and other women have done so. In doing so, I have had to face up to the idea that maybe others deserve such compassion also. Ministers can apologise, and I am sure that for some this is very important, the Church as an organisation can apologise, and for some this is an imperative. I know that the apologies I received from the individual nuns and priests I spoke to in All Hallows on behalf of their Church meant more to me than any corporate apology. It is only in taking out the ghosts of the past, resurrecting the bones of our stories, and breathing the spirit of our own voice into them that the truth will be fully understood. Only the voices of the women and children involved can bring those particular bones back to life. I have resurrected my story; I have trawled through the ghosts of my past and returned with my story. I have left the story of a cruel dictatorship of Church and State behind, where it belongs.